NEURO LINGUISTIC PROGRAMMING
Psychology for everyone

by
Kateryna Kolesnikovych

CONTENTS

PART 1: MINDSET and PSYCHOLOGICAL SELF-HELP THROUGH NLP

Chapter 1: Introduction to NLP
1.1 What to expect from NLP?..6
1.2 Brain usage manual..8
1.3 Pressupotions of NLP..12

Chapter 2: The Power of Mindset
2.1 The role of belief..16
2.2 Overcoming Limiting Beliefs..18
2.3 Programming Your Mind for Success..................................21

Chapter 3: NLP and Self-Awareness
3.1 The Meta Model: A Tool for Clarity....................................24
3.2 VAKOG: Sensory Acuity and Representation Systems......26
3.3 The Johari Window: Understanding Self and Others........31

Chapter 4: Techniques for Self-Help
4.1 Reframing: Changing Your Perspective................................34
4.2 Anchoring: Instilling Positive States....................................36
4.3 Visualisation and Future Pacing for Success......................38

Chapter 5: Emotional Mastery
5.1 Recognising and Managing Emotions................................41
5.2 The Swish Pattern: Modifying Behaviors............................42
5.3 Building Resilience with NLP..42

PART 2: NLP in COMMUNICATION ACROSS DIFFERENT LEVELS

Chapter 6: Internal Dialogue and Self-Talk
6.1 The Inner Voice: Understanding and Improving Self-Talk
....46

6.2 Strategies for Positive Self-Communication........................49
6.3 Dissolving Negative Self-Talk Patterns...............................52

Chapter 7: NLP in Personal Relationships
7.1 Is it fair?..55
7.2 Rapport Building, Mirroring and Matching Techniques........56
7.3 Conflict Resolution through NLP..60

Chapter 8: Romantic Relationships and NLP
8.1 Deepening Intimacy with Meta Programs............................63
8.2 The Love Strategies: Understanding Partners' Needs........67
8.3 NLP for Healing and Growth in Relationships....................68

Chapter 9: NLP in the Workplace
9.1 Effective Communication Strategies....................................71
9.2 Negotiation and Persuasion Techniques..............................72
9.3 Leadership and Team-Building through NLP......................73

Chapter 10: Advanced Communication Techniques
10.1 The Milton Model: Persuasive Language Patterns...........74
10.2 Meta Programs: Understanding People's Motivations.........75
10.3 Utilising Presuppositions for Influence................................75

PART 3: SELF-TRANSFORMATION and ACHIEVING GOALS THROUGH NLP

Chapter 11: Goal Setting with NLP
11.1 SMART Goals and Beyond An NLP Approach................78
11.2 The Well-Formed Outcome: A Blueprint for Success......78
11.3 Overcoming Obstacles and Maintaining Motivation......79

Chapter 12: Transforming Habits with NLP
12.1 Identifying and Changing Limiting Habits........................80
12.2 Installing New, Empowering Habits..................................82
12.3 The Role of Ecology in Habit Change...............................84

Chapter 13: NLP Strategies for Personal Change
13.1 The Change Personal History Technique..........85
13.2 Submodalities for Shifting Experience..........88
13.3 The New Behavior Generator..........89

Chapter 14: Modeling Excellence
14.1 The NLP Strategy for Modeling Success..........92
14.2 Case Studies of Successful Modeling..........93
14.3 Creating Your Pathway to Excellence..........93

Chapter 15: Integration and Continuous Improvement
15.1 Integrating NLP into Daily Life..........94
15.2 Continuous Improvement through NLP Practices..........96
15.3 Developing a Personal NLP Growth Plan..........97

CONCLUSION: THE NLP JOURNEY
Recap of Key Learnings..........100
Staying Engaged with NLP..........101
Next Steps and Resources..........101

88 ANTI MANIPULATION TECHNIQUES..........102

PART 1
Mindset and Psychological Self-Help through NLP

Chapter 1: Introduction to NLP

1.1 What to expect from NLP?

The Transformative Power of NLP

As you turn these pages, I invite you to step into a realm of transformation that defies clichés. NLP isn't a magical cure or a mere collection of theories – it is a gateway to profound change that stems from the most potent resource you possess: your mind.

Expect from NLP not a promise of an easy path but the tools to navigate the complexities of life with grace and tenacity. Each technique and exercise is a stepping stone towards surviving and thriving amidst challenges.

Like most people, I have used these methods for years for my goals in different areas of life, to introduce the proper habits leading to a healthy and beautiful body, for better relationships, thanks to the specific attention to those who are dear to me and in business process solutions.

But one day, all these goals were replaced by the task of survival. A war started in my country, and I had to use NLP techniques to stabilise my psycho-emotional reaction to what was happening. This is probably why I have written this book: I understand that if such practical psychology helped me be stress-resistant, everyone should understand its basics and support themselves in crucial tasks.

I am writing this book from London and being grateful to the people in my path and to the NLP techniques. In any difficult situation and cases requiring change, we need to have a certain mindset to launch processes leading to improving the situation. We also need correct communication with ourselves and others and actions, so three parts of this book are about thoughts, communication and actions.

A New Lens: The Expectations at Every Level of NLP Mastery

As we venture into the intricate and profound world of Neuro-Linguistic Programming (NLP), we recognise that learners at every stage bring unique perspectives and aspirations. Whether you are a newcomer to NLP or a seasoned practitioner, this journey offers a transformative experience, reshaping how you perceive and interact with the world around you.

For those just beginning to explore the realms of NLP and psychology, you stand at the threshold of a significant cognitive shift. NLP isn't merely a set of tools; it's a paradigm shift, transforming mundane thought patterns into a rich tapestry of insights and possibilities. As you delve deeper, your perception of the world will remain unchanged, yet your interpretation of it will be irrevocably altered. Everyday situations, challenges, and reflective moments become fertile ground for intellectual and personal growth.

Experienced individuals with a foundational understanding of psychological principles will discover a robust framework to enhance and refine their knowledge of NLP. NLP provides a structured approach to apply your skills with greater precision and impact. It's akin to an artist who, already proficient in basic techniques, learns to combine and layer these skills to create more nuanced and impactful works.

For coaches and therapists, NLP is an invaluable addition to your toolkit. It refines your ability to facilitate transformative change and empower growth in those you guide. NLP equips you with advanced strategies to uncover new perspectives and solutions, elevating your ability to effect meaningful change in your client's lives.

Regardless of your starting point, NLP will meet you at your current level and guide you towards uncharted personal and professional development territories. It's a path marked by continuous learning, skill enhancement, and the unending pursuit of growth.

The true power of NLP lies in its practical application. The transformations you seek, whether in personal growth, professional development, or achieving specific goals, are not merely aspirational. They are attainable milestones on your journey with NLP. Your ambitions are within reach, your goals achievable, and your potential is boundless.

As you engage with NLP, you will learn to master the language of your mind, navigate through your fears, and orchestrate your thoughts with purpose and precision. Prepare for a journey that promises theoretical knowledge and tangible, impactful, and life-altering experiences.

Welcome to an immersive world where change is not just a theoretical possibility but a tangible reality. Welcome to the transformative journey of NLP mastery.

1.2 Brain Usage Manual - Operating the Epicenter of Your Thoughts

Welcome to the control room of your existence: your brain. This is a different appliance with a three-page manual in twelve languages. Oh no. It's the ultimate supercomputer, and guess what? You're the CEO, the operator, and the maintenance crew. So, let's roll up our mental sleeves and get to work.

SECTION 1: CEO of Thought Inc.

First things first, you're in charge. Are those thoughts buzzing around like busy bees? You're responsible for them. Sure, the brain generates thoughts as the heart beats, but you decide which thoughts get promoted to actions and which ones get the pink slip. It's about taking charge and not just passively observing your mental chatter.

Exercise: Thought Audit

- Set a timer for 5 minutes and jot down every thought that comes to mind on a piece of paper. There are no filters; just write.

- Once the time is up, review the list and categorise each thought as *"productive," "unproductive,"* or *"neutral."*

- For every "unproductive" thought, write a counteractive *"productive"* thought next to it.

- Reflect on the pattern of your thoughts. Decide which 'unproductive' thoughts you're ready to 'fire' and which 'productive' thoughts you want to 'promote.'

SECTION 2: Mindset Renovation

Change starts in the fertile ground of the mind. It's like prepping a garden; you don't just throw seeds on concrete and hope for the best. You till you toil, you plant. Then you nurture. The same goes for your goals and dreams. The mindset you cultivate determines the bounty you'll harvest. Want change? Start with the soil of your soul and plant seeds of positivity and possibility.

Exercise: Planting the Seeds of Change

- Draw a large empty circle representing your 'garden on a sheet of paper.'

- Write down all the qualities or habits you wish to cultivate inside the circle.

- For each item, think of a small daily action or affirmation aligning with it and write it beside your 'garden.'

- Commit to daily practising these actions or affirmations to nurture your 'garden.'

SECTION 3: Mind Detox – Clearing Out the Cobwebs

Time for some mental decluttering. Our brains often hold onto old beliefs and ideas like a garage hoarding treasures from the "90s – nostalgic but not exactly useful. Some of these beliefs are hand-me-downs from previous generations, like that neon windbreaker from your Uncle Bob. It's time to thank them for their service and send them on their way. This is *"mind detox"*: evaluating what mental content serves you and kindly showing the door to what doesn't.

So, how do you detox? Start by identifying the junk – pessimistic patterns, outdated assumptions, and second-hand fears. Then, consciously choose to replace them with fresh, empowering thoughts. It's like updating your mental software. Sure, the 'Family Tradition 1.0 software had its time, but maybe 'Personal Growth 2.0' has those snazzy features you now need.

> **Exercise: Belief Decluttering**
>
> - Make a two-column list. In the first column, write down beliefs or ideas you've 'inherited' from family, society, etc.
> - In the second column, write whether it's a 'keep,' 'discard,' or 'update.'
> - For each 'discard' or 'update,' write a more relevant belief that better serves your current life.
> - Practice this by affirming the new beliefs every morning for a week.

SECTION 4: Thought Patterns – Updating Cognitive Frameworks

In cognitive development, understanding and updating our thought patterns is essential for adapting to the rapidly evolving demands of modern life. While our brains are inherently capable of remarkable adaptability, specific entrenched thought patterns, possibly effective in previous generations, may no longer benefit today's complex environment. This section aims to provide a more contemporary approach to cognitive processing, aligning our mental habits with current needs and goals.

The Neuroscience of Thought Patterns

1. **Neural Plasticity:** Modern neuroscience has shown that our brains exhibit plasticity, meaning they can change and adapt throughout our lives. This plasticity allows us to rewire and develop new, more practical thought patterns.
2. **Cognitive Ruts:** Often, repeated thoughts and behaviours can create neural pathways that become default modes of thinking. While these 'cognitive ruts' might have once been adaptive, they can become limiting in new contexts.
3. **Updating Cognitive Software:** We can reprogram our thought patterns, like updating software on a computer. This involves identifying outdated modes of thinking and consciously practising new, more adaptive thought processes.

Exercise: Mental Wardrobe Update

To modernise your cognitive framework, engage in an exercise I call the 'Mental Wardrobe Update.'

1. **Identification and Analysis:** Start by identifying outdated thought patterns. What are the recurring thoughts or beliefs that no longer serve you well? Analyse why these patterns may have developed and their current impact on your behaviour and decision-making.
2. **Designing New Patterns:** Next, determine what new thought patterns would be more beneficial. These should be based on current personal and professional goals and the latest understanding of effective mental habits.

Introduction to NLP

3. **Implementation and Practice:** Focus on implementing these new patterns. This requires conscious effort. Each time you fall back into old ways of thinking, actively shift to the new pattern. This might involve affirmations, mindfulness practices, or situational re-assessments.

4. **Evaluation:** Regularly evaluate how these new thought patterns affect your behaviour and mindset. Are they helping you to be more effective in your personal and professional life? Adjust as necessary based on these reflections.

1.3 Pressupotions of NLP

In NLP, presuppositions serve as the philosophical underpinning, shaping both the mindset and approach of practitioners and clients alike. They play a crucial role in establishing a framework for effective communication, ensuring that interactions are grounded in empathy and respect for individual perspectives. These guiding beliefs encourage a reorientation of thought processes, promoting a flexible and resourceful mindset that views challenges as opportunities for growth and learning. The presuppositions also directly influence the development and application of NLP techniques, underpinning strategies such as reframing and utilising internal resources. By fostering a growth-oriented and positive mindset, they create an empowering environment conducive to personal and professional development.

1. The Map is Not the Territory

Explanation: *Our perceptions of the world are not the world itself but merely our individual interpretation of it.*

Exercise: For one day, question your assumptions about a routine event or interaction. Write down what you believe to be true about it, then explore how others might see it differently.

2. **Respect for the Other Person's Model of the World**

   Explanation: *Each person's view of the world is valid, and honouring that perspective is essential.*

   Exercise: When conversing with someone, practice active listening without judgment. Repeat back their point of view to ensure you understand it fully before responding.

3. **Behavior and Change are to be Evaluated in Terms of Context and Ecology**

   Explanation: *Behaviors are neither good nor bad in themselves; their value depends on the context and the overall well-being they produce.*

   Exercise: Reflect on a behaviour you want to change. Consider when it might be helpful and how changing it could affect your life holistically.

4. **Resistance in a Client is a Sign of a Lack of Rapport**

   Explanation: *Resistance usually indicates a lack of connection or trust.*

   Exercise: If you encounter resistance, change your approach. Experiment with mirroring the other person's body language to build rapport.

5. **People are Not Their Behaviors**

   Explanation: *Accept the person, even if you choose not to accept their behaviour.*

   Exercise: Think of a behaviour you dislike in someone close to you. Separate the behaviour from the person and express appreciation for them apart from that behaviour.

6. **Everyone is Doing the Best They Can with the Resources They Have**

   Explanation: *People operate with the skills and knowledge available to them at the time.*

   Exercise: Reflect on a past mistake and list the resources or knowledge you have now that you didn't have then.

7. **The Person with the Most Flexibility Controls the System**

   Explanation: *Being adaptable in your behaviour gives you the most influence in any situation.*

   Exercise: Practice adjusting your communication style to match others' preferences in a group setting and observe the results.

8. **Mind and Body are Parts of the Same System**

   Explanation: *Your thoughts and physical state are interconnected.*

   Exercise: Engage in a physical activity and notice how it affects your mood and thinking.

9. **The Process of Communication is Not Just What You Say but Also How You Say It**

   Explanation: *Non-verbal cues often communicate more than words.*

   Exercise: With a friend, have a conversation using only non-verbal communication and see how much you can convey.

10. **We Have All the Resources We Need, or We Can Create Them**

    Explanation: *Solutions are often within ourselves, or we have the capacity to develop them.*

    Exercise: List five past challenges and the resources you used or developed to overcome them.

11. **There is Only Feedback, No Failure**

    Explanation: *Every result offers valuable information for growth and learning.*

    Exercise: Replace the word 'failure' with 'feedback' in your vocabulary for one week and note any shifts in perspective.

12. **The Meaning of Communication is the Response You Get**

    Explanation: *Effective communication is judged by the response it elicits, not by its intent.*

    Exercise: If a conversation doesn't go as intended, try a different way of communicating your message instead of blaming the other person.

13. Law of Requisite Variety

Explanation: *In any system, the element with the most flexibility will be the most influential.*

Exercise: When faced with a problem at work or home, brainstorm three ways to address it and choose the best approach.

14. People Have All the Resources They Need to Make Positive Changes

Explanation: *Within us, we have the necessary capabilities to change; it's a matter of accessing and mobilising them.*

Exercise: Identify a change you wish to make and list internal resources (traits, skills, experiences) that can aid in this change.

15. All Procedures Should Increase Wholeness

Explanation: *NLP interventions should aim to integrate rather than segment a person's experience.*

Exercise: Consider a change you're making and ensure it's congruent with all areas of your life, enhancing overall harmony.

Chapter 2: The Power of Mindset

2.1 The role of belief

> **Quick Exercise:** Uncovering the Impact of Beliefs
>
> **Objective:** To help you recognise how your beliefs shape your life
>
> 1. **Identify a Personal Belief:** Write down a belief you have about yourself, such as *"I'm not good at math."*
>
> 2. **Reflect on Impact:** Think about how this belief has influenced your actions. Have you avoided situations that involve math?
>
> 3. **Consequences:** Consider the outcomes of these actions. Did avoiding math limit your career or educational choices?
>
> 4. **Formulate a Positive Belief:** Create an alternative, empowering belief, like *"I can improve my math skills with practice."*
>
> 5. **Visualize a New Reality:** Imagine how this new belief could change your actions and open up new opportunities.
>
> 6. **Reflect:** Note any insights or feelings about how your original belief might have shaped your life's experiences.

As an NLP coach, I can provide insights into the role of beliefs in the framework of Neuro-Linguistic Programming.

In NLP, beliefs are considered incredibly powerful and play a central role in shaping our reality. Here are some key aspects of how beliefs function within the NLP perspective:

1. **Framework for Perception:** Beliefs act as filters through which we perceive the world. They shape our understanding and interpretation of experiences, effectively colouring how we see and interact with our environment and with others.
2. **Determinants of Behavior:** Our beliefs deeply influence our behaviour. For instance, if someone believes they are inherently unskilled in public speaking, they are likely to avoid situations that require them to speak in front of an audience. Changing this belief can open up new behaviours and opportunities.
3. **Self-Fulfilling Prophecies:** Beliefs can create self-fulfilling prophecies. If you believe you will succeed or fail at a particular endeavour, your actions, consciously or unconsciously, will often align to make that belief a reality.
4. **Influence on Emotional and Physical States:** Beliefs can impact our emotional and physical well-being. Negative beliefs can lead to stress, anxiety, and even physical health issues, while positive beliefs can promote emotional resilience and physical health.
5. **Guiding Values and Decisions:** Beliefs form the basis of our values and decision-making processes. They influence what we deem necessary, how we react in certain situations, and the choices we make on a day-to-day basis.
6. **Change and Growth:** In NLP, changing limiting beliefs is crucial for personal growth and development. By identifying and transforming beliefs that hold us back, we can unlock our potential and achieve tremendous success and fulfilment.
7. **Empowerment:** Empowering beliefs can significantly enhance a person's capabilities and experiences. Beliefs like *"I am capable of learning and growing"* or *"I can overcome challenges"* are seen as fuel for personal empowerment.

In NLP coaching, a significant part of the process involves helping clients identify their limiting beliefs, understand their origins, and reframe or replace them with more empowering beliefs.

This is often done through various techniques like reframing, visualisation, and the use of metaphor, aiming to create lasting positive change in the individual's life.

In a world where technology and digital interactions shape much of our daily lives, our belief systems play a pivotal role in navigating challenges and opportunities. Limiting beliefs, those negative assumptions we hold about ourselves and our capabilities, can hinder personal and professional growth. However, with the right strategies, especially ones tailored for the digital age, overcoming these beliefs is not just possible but can be an engaging and transformative journey.

Limiting beliefs are often deeply ingrained thoughts that originate from past experiences, societal influences, or even familial teachings. They act as mental barriers, preventing us from pursuing goals, trying new things, or taking risks. Common examples include beliefs like "I'm not good enough," "I can't achieve success," or "I don't deserve happiness."

2.2 Overcoming Limiting Beliefs

Overcoming limiting beliefs is a multi-step process that involves self-awareness, challenging existing thought patterns, and adopting new, more empowering beliefs. Here's a detailed look at how this process typically unfolds:

1. **Identify Limiting Beliefs:** The first step is to become aware of your limiting beliefs. These are often deeply ingrained and can surface through introspection, feedback from others, or during challenging situations.

2. **Understand Their Origins:** Once you've identified these beliefs, try to understand where they come from. Often, limiting beliefs originate from past experiences, societal messages, or things we were taught in childhood. Understanding the root of these beliefs is crucial for addressing them effectively.

3. **Challenge the Beliefs:** question and challenge these beliefs. Ask yourself whether they are objectively true or if there's evidence that contradicts them. For example, you can look for instances where you have succeeded or been competent if you need to improve.

4. **Reframe the Beliefs:** Use reframing techniques to alter how you perceive these beliefs. This involves looking at the belief differently or finding a positive angle. For instance, instead of seeing failure as a negative reflection of your abilities, view it as an opportunity for growth and learning.

5. **Adopt New, Empowering Beliefs:** Replace the old, limiting beliefs with new, positive ones. If your limiting belief was "I can't achieve success," an empowering belief could be "I am capable of achieving success through hard work and dedication."

6. **Visualization and Affirmations:** Regularly visualise yourself acting and thinking in ways that reflect your new beliefs. Use affirmations to reinforce these beliefs in your daily life.

7. **Behavioral Changes:** Start to act in ways that align with your new beliefs. This might involve taking on new challenges, changing how you interact with others, or altering your daily habits.

8. **Seek Support:** Don't hesitate to seek support from friends, mentors, or professionals like therapists or coaches. They can provide guidance, perspective, and encouragement as you work through this process.

9. **Monitor Progress and Adapt:** Regularly reflect on your progress. Are you finding it more accessible to act in ways that align with your new beliefs? Do certain situations still trigger your old beliefs? Please just adapt your approach as needed based on your observations and experiences.

10. **Persistence and Patience:** Changing deeply held beliefs takes time and persistence. Be patient with yourself and recognise that it's a process. Celebrate small victories and stay committed to your growth.

The Power of Mindset

Following these steps, you can systematically work through and overcome limiting beliefs, paving the way for a more empowered and fulfilling life.

Now let's walk through an example of how someone can overcome the limiting belief, *"You have to do it yourself if you want it done well,"* especially when aiming to delegate more effectively.

1. **Identify the Limiting Belief:** John recognises he has difficulty delegating tasks as a team manager. He identifies his limiting belief as *"I need to do everything myself for it to be done correctly."*

2. **Understand Its Origins:** Reflecting on his past, John realises this belief stems from early career experiences where he felt his success depended solely on his efforts. Over time, this belief became ingrained in his approach to work.

3. **Challenge the Belief:** John starts questioning this belief by looking at evidence to the contrary. He notices colleagues who delegate effectively and achieve excellent results. He also acknowledges instances where his direct involvement was optional for a task's success.

4. **Reframe the Belief:** John begins to reframe his belief. He says, *"Delegating tasks can lead to high-quality outcomes and helps develop my team's skills."*

5. **Adopt New, Empowering Beliefs:** John adopts a new belief: *"My team is capable, and delegating tasks is an effective way to manage our workload and grow collectively."*

6. **Visualization and Affirmations:** John visualises a successful workday each morning where he delegates tasks effectively and sees positive outcomes. He uses affirmations like, *"I trust my team and value their contributions."*

7. **Behavioral Changes:** John starts small, delegating minor tasks and gradually increasing to more significant responsibilities. He observes how his team handles these tasks, reinforcing his new belief.

8. **Seek Support:** John discusses his goal of delegating more with a mentor, who provides advice and reassurance, reinforcing that delegation is a critical skill for leadership.

9. **Monitor Progress and Adapt:** Over time, John regularly reflects on his experiences with delegation. He notes improvements in his team's abilities and his own comfort with delegating.

10. **Persistence and Patience:** Although initially challenging, John remains patient and persistent. He celebrates small milestones, like a week of successful delegation, and stays committed to changing his approach.

Through this process, John can overcome his limiting beliefs, becoming a more effective manager who can delegate tasks confidently, knowing that it contributes positively to the team's development and success.

2.3 Programming Your Mind for Success

Your mind is the most powerful tool, and how you program it can significantly impact your life. In Neuro-Linguistic Programming (NLP), we explore various strategies to harness this power. This chapter delves into practical ways to reprogram your mind, guided by wisdom from some renowned NLP trainers.

1. Believe in What Benefits You

"Beliefs have the power to create and the power to destroy." - Tony Robbins, an acclaimed NLP expert, emphasises the power of belief. If you're going to believe in something, make sure it serves you positively. This doesn't mean ignoring reality but choosing to believe in perspectives that empower and motivate you.

2. Focus on What You Need and What You Can Do

Richard Bandler, one of the founders and inventors of NLP, advises focusing on actionable and beneficial goals. It's crucial to concentrate on what you need and your capacity to achieve it. This means setting realistic goals and recognising your strengths.

> **Exercise:** Goal Visualization
> - Write down a specific goal.
> - Visualise achieving this goal, focusing on the steps you can take.
> - Each day, take a small action towards this goal.

3. The Power of Positive Language

Another NLP co-founder, John Grinder, highlights language's importance in shaping our thoughts and actions. Using positive, empowering language can significantly influence your mindset and behaviour.

> **Exercise:** Language Awareness
> - Pay attention to your language for a day.
> - Replace negative phrases with positive ones.
> - Notice how this changes your mood and interactions.

4. Model Excellence

Tony Robbins also champions the concept of modelling - observing and emulating the qualities of those who excel in areas you wish to improve. You can incorporate these elements into your life by studying their behaviours, beliefs, and strategies.

> **Exercise:** Excellence Analysis
> - Choose a role model who embodies your desired success.
> - Research and list their key habits and beliefs.
> - Implement one habit or belief into your routine.

5. Embrace Change

Both Bandler and Grinder agree that flexibility and adaptability are key to success. Embracing change and being willing to adjust your strategies is crucial in the dynamic landscape of life.

> **Exercise:** Flexibility Challenge
> - Identify an area where you're resistant to change.
> - For one week, try a new approach in this area.
> - Reflect on the experience and what you learned.

Programming your mind effectively is a cornerstone of NLP. You can unlock your full potential by adopting beliefs that benefit you, focusing on achievable goals, using positive language, modelling excellence, and embracing change. Remember, your thoughts' quality largely determines your life's quality. Harness them wisely.

Chapter 3: NLP and Self-Awareness

This chapter unveils the layers of self-awareness through NLP tools and models. It's not just about knowing yourself but understanding how you interact with the world.

3.1 The Meta Model: A Tool for Clarity

The Meta Model, a fundamental aspect of NLP, introduced by Richard Bandler and John Grinder, serves as a linguistic toolkit to enhance clarity and understanding in communication. It's designed to challenge and expand the often limited representation of our experiences through language.

The Essence of The Meta Mode

At its core, the Meta Model helps us to:

- **Uncover Underlying Beliefs:** It reveals our communication's hidden beliefs and assumptions.
- **Clarify Vague Language:** It addresses generalisations, deletions, and distortions in our speech.
- **Enhance Mutual Understanding:** By seeking specificity it fosters more transparent and effective communication.

The Components of The Meta Model

The Meta Model consists of specific questioning techniques:

- **Challenging Generalizations:** Questions like *"Always? Every time?"* can unpack sweeping statements.
- **Exploring Deletions:** Queries like *"What specifically?"* can fill in the missing information.

- Clarifying Distortions: Asking *"How exactly does this cause that?"* can address causal assumptions.

Application in Everyday Life

In Personal Conversations:

- **Situation:** Your friend says, *"Nobody cares about me."*
- **Meta Model Response:** *"Who specifically do you feel doesn't care about you?"*
- **Outcome:** This encourages your friend to reconsider their statement's absolute nature and identify specific concerns, making it easier to address them.

In Business Communications:

- **Situation:** A colleague remarks, *"This project is going nowhere."*
- **Meta Model Response:** *"What specifically is causing the project to stall?"*
- **Outcome:** This question helps to identify specific issues with the project, leading to a more focused discussion on solutions.

Application in Problem-Solving. Case Study:

- **Scenario:** A team member states, *"We can't complete this task because we're not skilled enough."*
- **Meta-Model Approach:** *"What specific skills do you think we are missing? How can we acquire or develop these skills?"*
- **Impact:** This approach moves the conversation from a generalised limitation to identifying specific skill gaps and solutions, fostering a growth mindset.

The Meta Model is a powerful tool that goes beyond mere conversation. It is about peeling back the layers of everyday language to reveal deeper meanings and beliefs. By mastering this model, you can enhance your personal relationships, improve professional communication, and become a more effective problem-solver. It's not just about asking questions; it's about opening doors to a deeper understanding and connection.

> **Exercise:** Question Your Questions
> - Next time you're in a conversation, listen for generalisations, deletions, or distortions in speech.
> - Politely ask clarifying questions like, *"How specifically?"* or *"What exactly do you mean?"*
> - Notice how these questions bring more clarity and understanding to the conversation.

3.2 VAKOG: Sensory Acuity and Representation Systems

Engage Your Senses

VAKOG stands for Visual, Auditory, Kinesthetic, Olfactory, and Gustatory. It's about understanding how you and others experience the world through these senses. We each have a preferred sensory system for processing information, which shapes our experiences and memories.

In the realm of NLP, the concept of VAKOG, which stands for Visual, Auditory, Kinesthetic, Olfactory, and Gustatory, plays a pivotal role in understanding how individuals process information and experience the world around them. Typically, people tend to have one or two dominant representational systems that they lean on more heavily, although they do utilise all of these systems to a certain extent.

Those who are visually oriented often think in pictures and are particularly sensitive to visual cues. Their language is peppered with phrases that reflect this, such as *"I see what you mean"* or

"Look at it this way." Meanwhile, auditory-focused individuals might think in terms of sounds and are more attuned to the nuances of voice tones. They will likely use expressions like *"I hear you"* or *"That sounds right to me."* Kinesthetic individuals, on the other hand, process their world through feelings and physical sensations. They often express themselves with phrases like *"I grasp the concept"* or *"I can't get a handle on this."*

While olfactory (smell) and gustatory (taste) are less common as primary systems in daily interactions, they are still part of the spectrum. Phrases like *"This situation stinks"* or *"That leaves a bad taste in my mouth"* can sometimes be heard, although they are often used metaphorically.

One effective method to identify a person's leading representational system is to listen carefully to their language and the phrases they use. This can offer clear indicators of their preferred mode of processing. Observing eye movements can also provide insights; in NLP, it's believed that specific eye movements correspond with accessing different types of thoughts. For example, people looking upward are often considered visual thinkers; sideways movements may indicate auditory processing, and downward glances might suggest kinesthetic thinking.

Paying attention to what individuals focus on in their environment can also be revealing. Those with a visual preference might comment on visual aspects like colours or designs, while auditory individuals might be more responsive to sounds or tones. Kinesthetic people might focus more on the feel or comfort of their surroundings.

Additionally, the types of gestures people use can hint at their dominant representational system. Visual people often gesture upwards or in front of them, indicating their visually oriented thought processes. In contrast, auditory individuals might gesture towards their ears, and kinesthetic individuals may use broader body gestures or engage in physical touch.

Finally, observing how people respond to different types of

communication can be quite telling. Visual individuals might be more responsive to visual demonstrations, auditory individuals to spoken explanations, and kinesthetic individuals to hands-on experiences.

In summary, understanding a person's preferred representational system is not just about enhancing communication; it's about connecting with them on a deeper level. This knowledge allows for adapting communication styles to align with their preferred mode, fostering more effective and meaningful interactions. It's essential, however, to remember that while individuals may show preferences, they are not confined to them and can operate across all representational systems, significantly when context and circumstances vary.

> **Exercise:** Sensory Journey
> - For one day, focus on one sense at a time for an hour. Observe how you experience the world through that sense alone.
> - Write down your observations and reflect on which senses you favour and how they influence your perception of events.

In addition to the VAKOG (Visual, Auditory, Kinesthetic, Olfactory, and Gustatory) representational systems, some people prefer a more analytical and logical way of processing information. These individuals are often referred to as having a "Digital" (or Auditory Digital) representational system.

People with a dominant digital or auditory digital style tend to process the world more rationally, analytically, and structuredly. They are often focused on facts, data, and logical reasoning. This style is less about sensory experience (like seeing, hearing, or feeling) and more about internal dialogue, categorisation, and evaluation.

Characteristics of individuals with a digital representational system include:

> **Preference for Logical Analysis:** They enjoy breaking down information into components, analysing data, and making decisions based on logical reasoning.
> **Structured Thinking:** They often have a systematic approach to thinking and problem-solving.
> **Internal Dialogue:** They may engage in extensive internal dialogue, constantly thinking, comparing, and evaluating information.
> **Language Usage:** Their language tends to be precise, often incorporating technical or specialised vocabulary. They use phrases like *"I understand the facts," "Let's analyse this,"* or *"According to the data."*

Identifying and understanding someone's preference for a digital representational system can be particularly helpful in contexts like business, academics, and technical fields, where analytical thinking and data-driven decision-making are prevalent. Communicating with individuals with this preference often involves presenting information in a structured, logical manner, backing up arguments with facts and data, and engaging in intellectual discussions.

Recognising this style can help tailor communication and interaction strategies to match their way of processing information, thus enhancing understanding and collaboration.

Here's a practical exercise explicitly designed to enhance analytical and logical thinking:

Exercise: Logical Perspectives

Objective: To strengthen analytical thinking and rational decision-making skills.

Step 1: Identify a Situation or Problem
Choose a current situation or problem you are facing. It could be a work-related issue, a personal decision, or any scenario requiring thought and analysis.

Step 2: Fact-Finding
Begin by gathering all the facts and data related to the situation. Write them down in a structured format. Focus on obtaining objective, concrete information that is not influenced by emotions or subjective judgments.

Step 3: Analyze the Information
Examine the facts you have collected. Look for patterns, inconsistencies, or any insights that can be drawn from the data. Use logical reasoning to analyse the information. You might consider creating lists, tables, or flowcharts to organise and visualise the data more effectively.

Step 4: Explore Different Perspectives
Consider the situation from multiple viewpoints. List the logical outcomes, potential impacts, and pros and cons for each perspective. This step involves rational analysis to understand the problem from various angles, not just your initial viewpoint.

Step 5: Internal Dialogue and Evaluation
Engage in a structured internal dialogue. Challenge yourself to think critically about the situation. Ask questions like, *"What is the most logical course of action?"* or *"What does the data suggest is the best solution?"*

Step 6: Make a Decision
Based on your analysis, make a decision that seems most logical and well-founded. Write down the rationale behind your decision to reinforce the analytical process.

Step 7: Reflect and Learn
After some time, reflect on the outcome of your decision. Consider what you learned from the exercise and how your analytical thinking influenced the result.

This exercise is designed to cater to the strengths of those with a Digital or Auditory Digital preference, emphasising logical analysis, structured thinking, and data-driven decision-making. However, it is also necessary for those who lack such skills and can be particularly beneficial in enhancing problem-solving skills and making well-informed decisions.

3.3 The Johari Window: Understanding Self and Others

The Mirror and the Window

The Johari Window is a framework that helps us understand our relationship with ourselves and others. It's like a window with four panes representing different aspects of our personality.

These panes are the Open Self, Hidden Self, Blind Self, and Unknown Self. Each represents elements known or unknown to us and to others.

The Four Quadrants of the Johari Window

1. Open Area (Open Self):

- This quadrant represents qualities and behaviours known to the individual and others.
- It includes information like attitudes, skills, and shared experiences.
- The open area can be expanded through disclosure and feedback.

2. Blind Area (Blind Self):

- This area contains information known to others but unknown to the individual.
- It might include habits or traits others see, but the person is unaware of.

NLP and Self-Awareness

> Increasing self-awareness and seeking feedback can help reduce the blind area.

3. Hidden Area (Hidden Self):

> The hidden quadrant represents information the individual knows about themselves but keeps hidden from others.
> This could include feelings, past experiences, fears, secrets, and private thoughts.
> Sharing and disclosing more personal information can enlarge the open area.

4. Unknown Area (Unknown Self):

> This quadrant covers information, abilities, feelings, and traits unknown to the individual and others.
> It could include latent talents, unconscious motives, or repressed memories.
> Exploration, experimentation, and feedback can help uncover these aspects.

Exercise: Self-Discovery Panes
- Draw your own Johari Window, labeling each pane.
- Fill in traits or aspects you think fit into each category.
- Share this with a trusted friend or family member and ask for their input, especially for the Blind Self section.

Importance in Personal Development

The Johari Window encourages people to reflect on different aspects of themselves. It aids in understanding what we reveal, don't reveal, and don't even know about ourselves.

We can communicate more effectively and authentically by understanding what we and others know about us.

The model helps build trust in relationships as more information moves into the open area through disclosure and feedback.

The Johari Window is a dynamic tool; as we grow and receive feedback, the size of the different quadrants changes. It encourages openness and honesty with oneself and others.

The Johari Window, developed in 1955 by Joseph Luft and Harrington Ingham, remains a relevant and widely used model in the fields of psychology, organisational development, and team building, offering a clear and straightforward framework for introspection, improving interpersonal communication and fostering better understanding within groups.

Chapter 4: Techniques for Self-Help

Neuro-Linguistic Programming (NLP) offers a variety of self-help techniques that can be particularly useful in the fast-paced, digital world we live in. Here are some fundamental NLP techniques and how they can be applied for personal and business success:

4.1 Reframing: Changing Your Perspective

Alright, let's talk about reframing. It's like looking at the same picture but choosing to focus on a different part of it. The picture doesn't change, but your perspective does, and that can make all the difference.

For example, let's say you're working on a project at work and hit a roadblock. You might think, 'This is impossible; I can't do this.' That's a natural reaction, but it's not helping you, right? Now, let's reframe it. Instead of seeing it as an impossible barrier, you could think, 'This is a challenging puzzle, and I love puzzles. It's an opportunity to learn something new.' Feel the shift? You're still acknowledging the difficulty, but now you also see it as an exciting challenge.

Or, consider a personal example. Imagine you've planned a picnic, and it starts raining. Instead of dwelling on the ruined plan, reframe it as, 'Great, I get to experience a cosy indoor picnic.' See, it's not just about being positive; it's about finding new, empowering perspectives.

Reframing is powerful in both personal and professional settings. In business, especially in leadership roles, how you frame situations can impact you and your entire team. Your team might feel demotivated if you view a setback as a disaster. But if you see it as a learning opportunity, your team's mindset shifts too.

Remember, it's not about denying the negative aspects; it's about choosing also to see the positive possibilities. It's like having a mental toolbox. When you encounter a challenging situation, you open the toolbox and think, 'Which tool can help me view this differently?'

So, next time you face a challenge, pause and ask yourself, 'How else can I look at this? Is there a more empowering way to frame this situation?' It takes practice, but once you get the hang of it, you'll start noticing a positive change in your mindset and reactions.

Now that we understand the basics of reframing let's explore how you can apply this technique in various aspects of your life. The beauty of reframing is its versatility – it can be applied to almost any situation, personal, professional, or social.

Let's take a typical workplace scenario. Imagine leading a team, and a project you're working on must meet the deadline. The immediate, natural reaction might be frustration and disappointment. But let's reframe it. Ask yourself, 'What can we learn from this? How can this experience make us more efficient for future projects?' Suddenly, the 'failure' becomes a stepping stone for improvement.

Or consider a personal situation. Say you've been trying to get fit, but you're not seeing results as quickly as you'd hoped. It's easy to get discouraged and think, 'Why bother?' But let's reframe that thought. Think, 'Every small step I take contributes to my overall health. I'm playing the long game, and persistence is key.' This mindset keeps you motivated and focused on your long-term goal.

Here's another angle to reframing – dealing with criticism. Say your boss critiques your work. Instead of taking it personally and thinking, 'I'm not good enough,' reframe it to, 'This feedback is valuable. It's an opportunity to grow and excel in my role.' This approach turns a potentially harmful experience into a constructive one.

Now, let's talk about social situations. Imagine you're at a networking event, and you're not naturally outgoing. You might think, 'I don't fit in here.' Let's reframe that. Think, 'This is a chance to step out of my comfort zone and develop new skills.' This perspective empowers you to engage with others positively.

Reframing is also about acknowledging and changing your internal dialogues. We often have automatic negative thoughts that can hold us back. By consciously reframing these thoughts, we can significantly improve our mental well-being and overall outlook on life.

Lastly, remember that reframing is a skill; like any skill, it requires practice. Start small. Whenever you catch yourself having a negative thought, pause and ask, 'How can I see this differently?' Over time, this will become a natural part of your thought process, leading to more positivity and resilience in your life.

So, keep practising reframing. It's a simple yet powerful tool that can transform not just how you view situations but also how you live your life.

4.2 Anchoring: Instilling Positive States

Anchoring is another fascinating and practical technique in NLP. Let's dive into this concept with a more interactive, real-world approach, as if you're in a session with an NLP coach.

Here's the gist of it: Anchoring involves creating a link between a specific physical trigger and a desired emotional state. It's like when you hear a song that instantly takes you back to a happy moment or when a particular smell reminds you of a cherished place. We're going to create that link intentionally.

Let's start with an example. Think of a time when you felt incredibly confident – got it? As you're reliving that feeling, do something unique, like pressing your thumb and forefinger together or gently tapping your knee. This is your anchor. We're associating that peak feeling of confidence with this physical action.

Once you've established this anchor, you can use it whenever you need a boost of confidence. Let's say you're about to give a presentation and feel nervous. Activate your anchor – press your thumb and forefinger together. This action should help bring back that feeling of confidence as if you're triggering it on command.

Anchoring is wider than confidence. You can create anchors for emotions like calmness, joy, or motivation. The key is choosing a unique physical action for each emotion and establishing the anchor when you're experiencing that emotion intensely.

Now, a crucial part of anchoring is practice. The more you reinforce the anchor, the stronger it becomes. Regularly recall the positive state and activate your anchor. Over time, the response will become more automatic and potent.

In the business world, this can be incredibly useful. Imagine you're in a challenging meeting and need to remain calm and collected. Use your 'calm' anchor. It can help centre your emotions and keep you focused.

And remember, the beauty of anchoring is its subtlety. No one needs to know you're doing it. It's your personal tool to manage your emotional states, giving you an edge in various situations – from difficult conversations to high-pressure environments.

So, give anchoring a try. Identify the emotions you'd like to have on tap, establish your anchors when you're experiencing those emotions, and then practice. It's like having a secret weapon for emotional regulation and resilience.

4.3 Visualisation and Future Pacing for Success

Visualisation and Future Pacing are powerful techniques in NLP, often used to enhance personal and professional success. Alright, let's dive into Visualization and Future Pacing. These techniques are all about creating a mental blueprint for success. It's like building your future with your imagination.

Visualisation is straightforward. It involves vividly imagining achieving your goals. But it's not just about seeing it; it's about feeling it, experiencing it in your mind as if it's already happening. This process activates the same neural pathways as experiencing the event, making your brain 'practice' successful.

Here's how you can do it: Close your eyes and picture a goal you want to achieve. Let's say it's delivering a successful presentation. Visualise yourself standing confidently, speaking clearly, and the audience responding positively. Feel the confidence, hear the applause, see the smiles. Make it as authentic as possible in your mind. This mental rehearsal boosts your confidence and prepares you psychologically to perform well.

Now, "Future Pacing" takes visualisation a step further. It involves projecting yourself into the future after you've achieved your goal. Imagine it's a few hours after your successful presentation. You're feeling accomplished and proud. How does that feel? What are people saying to you? Future Pacing strengthens the neural pathways even more, creating a sense of inevitability about your success.

In business, visualisation and future pacing can be game-changers. Before a crucial meeting or decision, visualise the outcome you desire. See yourself navigating the meeting successfully, making the right decisions, and achieving the best possible result.

But remember, visualisation isn't just daydreaming. The key is to pair it with action. Visualise your success, then identify your steps to get there. This combination of mental rehearsal and practical action planning significantly increases your chances of success.

Moreover, these techniques can be a source of motivation and resilience. When facing challenges or setbacks, visualise overcoming them. This not only keeps you motivated but also helps in finding creative solutions.

So, start incorporating visualisation and future pacing into your routine. Whether for a small daily goal or a big future ambition, these techniques can help you prepare mentally, boost confidence, and pave the way for success.

And let's delve deeper into how Visualization and Future Pacing prepare you mentally and catalyse real-world action and planning.

It's crucial to understand that Visualization and Future Pacing are powerful tools but not magic wands. They set the stage, but the play is yours to perform. Think of them as blueprints, just as an architect doesn't just draw plans but also oversees their realisation; you, too, must act on the visions you create.

Let's expand on the earlier example of the presentation. When you visualise giving a successful presentation, you're not just fantasising. You're mentally preparing yourself. This mental rehearsal can highlight areas you need to work on. You may visualise a moment where you're stumbling over a particular presentation part. That's a signal – you need to prepare more on that part.

Now, about Future Pacing. When you imagine the aftermath of a successful presentation, you're not just basking in imaginary glory. You're setting a psychological expectation for yourself. This expectation can be a powerful motivator. It's like telling yourself, 'This is where I'm going to be, and here's what it'll feel like.' It builds a sense of purpose and direction.

But here's the crucial part – action. Visualisation and Future Pacing are most effective when they lead to action. After visualising success, ask yourself, 'What steps do I need to take to make this a reality?' Break it down. Maybe you need to research more, practice your speech, or get feedback from a colleague. Your visualisation becomes a roadmap for these actions.

In a broader sense, apply this to any goal. Visualise achieving it, then future pace to feel the success. Then, critically outline the steps to get there. What skills do you need to develop? What resources do you need? Who can help you?

This process also helps with overcoming obstacles. Visualise facing a challenge and navigating through it. This prepares your mind for potential hurdles and starts the process of finding solutions. Again, follow up with action plans. What will you do if you encounter this obstacle? What resources will you need to overcome it?

Remember, the brain sometimes struggles to distinguish between vivid visualisation and authentic experiences. By repeatedly visualizing success and its path, you're programming your brain to recognise these patterns as achievable and familiar. This familiarity breeds confidence, and confidence propels action.

So, practice visualisation and future pacing regularly. Use them to clarify your goals, prepare mentally, and, most importantly, catalyse actual, tangible actions towards achieving those goals. They are the starting blocks, but the race is run in the real world.

This explanation emphasises the practical aspects of Visualization and Future Pacing, highlighting their role in not just mental preparation but also in spurring actionable steps towards achieving your goals. Regularly engaging in these practices can enhance your readiness for future challenges and opportunities, leading to more effective planning and action in your journey towards success.

Chapter 5: Emotional Mastery

5.1 Recognizing and Managing Emotions.

In NLP, emotional recognition involves becoming aware of one's internal emotional states and understanding how these states influence behavior. This awareness is crucial because emotions are powerful drivers of thought and action.

Emotions can be viewed as a feedback system. They indicate how we interpret and react to various situations.

Whether positive or negative, each emotion serves a purpose and can offer insights into our beliefs and perceptions.

The goal is not to suppress emotions but to understand and channel them more productively.

Emotional mastery starts with awareness. It's about recognising your emotions and understanding their impact on your thoughts and behaviours. In NLP, this is often approached through self-reflection and mindfulness techniques.

> **Technique:** *Mindful Observation*
>
> **Practice:** Take time each day to observe your emotional state without judgment. Acknowledge what you're feeling and consider what might be triggering these emotions. This awareness is the first step in managing your feelings effectively.

> **Technique:** *State Management*
>
> **Practice:** Once you're aware of your emotions, you can start to manage them. Techniques like deep breathing, meditation, or

even physical exercise can help alter emotional states. The key is to find what works best for you in different situations.

5.2 The Swish Pattern: Modifying Behaviors

The Swish Pattern is an NLP technique that transforms negative or unproductive behaviour patterns into positive ones.

This technique is based on the principle that our behaviours are often linked to specific triggers and are reinforced through repetition. By visualising a negative behaviour and 'swishing' it with a positive one, we're effectively rewiring our brain's response to the trigger.

The repeated practice of the Swish Pattern helps to establish new neural pathways, facilitating behaviour change.

Description: It involves visualising the unwanted behaviour and then 'swishing' it with a desired behaviour. The process helps break the old pattern and establish a new, more beneficial one.

> **Example:** If you have a habit of procrastinating, visualise the scenario where you usually procrastinate. Then, immediately 'swish' this image with a visualisation of you taking immediate and confident action. Repeating this exercise can help rewire your response to the trigger.

5.3 Building Resilience with NLP

Building resilience involves developing the mental and emotional strength to handle challenges, stress, and adversity. NLP offers several techniques to enhance this ability.

Technique: *Reframing Negative Experiences*

Reframing is based on the idea that our interpretation of events, not the events themselves, dictates our emotional response.

We can alter our emotional and behavioural responses by consciously changing our perspective on a challenging situation.

Technique: *Anchoring Positive States*

Anchoring draws on the concept that emotional states can be triggered by specific stimuli (anchors).

By creating anchors during positive emotional states, we can later trigger these states on demand, which is invaluable during stressful or challenging times.

Technique: *Future Pacing for Resilience*

Future Pacing involves mentally rehearsing future scenarios where one successfully overcomes a challenge.

This technique is grounded in the idea that mental rehearsal can prepare the mind and body to respond more effectively in real-life situations.

Technique: *Reframing Negative Experiences*

Practice: Use reframing to view challenges as opportunities for growth. When faced with a setback, ask yourself what you can learn from this experience and how it can strengthen you.

Technique: *Anchoring Positive States*

Practice: Develop anchors for states like calmness and resilience. When you feel these emotions strongly, create a physical anchor (like touching your wrist). Use this anchor in tough times to bring back these positive states.

Technique: *Future Pacing for Resilience*

Practice: Visualize yourself handling a future challenge

Emotional Mastery

successfully and resiliently. The more vividly you can imagine this, the more prepared and resilient you'll feel when faced with real-life challenges.

Emotional mastery is not about never experiencing negative emotions; it's about recognising them, understanding them, and managing them to serve your well-being and goals. By practising techniques like the Swish Pattern, mindfulness, and anchoring, you can gain greater control over your emotional responses, leading to more effective behaviour patterns and increased resilience. Remember, like any skill, emotional mastery requires practice and patience. The more you work on it, the more adept you'll become at managing your emotions and responding to life's challenges with strength and flexibility.

PART 2
NLP in Communication Across Different Levels

Chapter 6: Internal Dialogue and Self-Talk

6.1 The Inner Voice: Understanding and Improving Self-Talk

The Role of Self-Talk in Communication and Success

Our internal dialogue, often called our *"inner voice"*, plays a crucial role in virtually every aspect of our lives. It influences how we communicate with others, our financial and career success, and our relationships as parents or partners. This self-talk can be a powerful tool if used positively, but it can also be a hindrance if it's negative or self-critical.

In Communication: Our inner voice shapes how we interpret interactions with others. Positive self-talk can boost our confidence, making us more effective communicators. Conversely, negative self-talk can lead to self-doubt, adversely affecting communication skills.

In Career and Financial Success: A constructive inner dialogue can drive motivation, resilience, and creativity, essential for career progression and financial success. It encourages a growth mindset, allowing us to see challenges as opportunities for growth rather than insurmountable obstacles.

In Personal Relationships: Whether as parents or partners, our internal dialogue influences our patience, empathy, and understanding. A nurturing inner voice can help us be more supportive and understanding, whereas a critical voice might lead to impatience and misunderstandings.

Everyday Processes of Self-Talk

Self-talk is a constant, almost subconscious process that significantly influences our daily lives. It typically occurs automatically and is often triggered by everyday situations. For example, challenges might elicit immediate thoughts like, "I can't do this," reflecting our instinctive self-talk. This internal dialogue is a reaction to events and reflects our mood.

When we're in a positive mood, our self-talk tends to be more optimistic, and conversely, a negative mood can lead to more critical or pessimistic self-talk. Self-talk is a way for our brain to process information, make sense of what's happening around us, and manage our emotions. It's deeply intertwined with our cognitive processes, helping us organise our thoughts, plan actions, and make decisions. Moreover, our self-talk often mirrors our deep-seated beliefs and attitudes. For instance, if we believe in our capabilities, our internal dialogue will likely be more encouraging.

Various factors influence the nature and tone of our self-talk. Past experiences play a crucial role; successes can lead to more affirmative self-talk, while past failures might result in a more negative internal monologue. The cultural and societal norms we are exposed to also shape our self-talk. Different cultures have different values, influencing whether our self-talk is modest or self-affirming. Additionally, the type of interpersonal relationships we have significantly affects our self-talk. Supportive and positive interactions foster encouraging self-talk, whereas critical or negative relationships can lead to a more detrimental internal dialogue. Mental health is another vital factor; conditions like depression or anxiety can skew self-talk towards the negative, often creating a challenging feedback loop. Understanding these influences can be critical to consciously directing our self-talk and improving our mental well-being, decision-making, and overall life experience.

Exercises to Improve Self-Talk

1. **Mindfulness and Awareness:** Start by becoming aware of your inner dialogue. Notice when it's negative and gently guide it towards a more positive tone.

2. **Affirmations:** Develop a set of positive affirmations that resonate with you. Repeat these daily to reinforce a positive mindset.

3. **Journaling:** Keep a journal to track your inner dialogue. Writing down your thoughts can help you understand and reframe them more positively.

4. **Gratitude Practice:** List three daily things you're grateful for. This practice can shift your focus from what's going wrong to what's going right.

5. **Cognitive Restructuring:** Challenge and replace negative thoughts with more realistic, positive alternatives. For instance, change *"I can't do this"* to *"I'll do the best I can."*

My primary approach is that you must notice what leads you to joy or some particular condition that makes you feel mixed emotions, such as confidence and happiness. For instance, you might feel perfect after or while doing sports, running with particular music in your earphones, or driving the car on an empty road. You have to do these as often as possible because you train for happiness this way, and some hours later, you are still in the condition of the champion. You can also set an anchor on the peak of such a moment and use this anchor for significant cases.

6.2 Strategies for Positive Self-Communication

Understanding and improving our inner dialogue can profoundly impact every aspect of our lives, from personal relationships to professional endeavours.

Real-Life Examples

Career Scenario: Imagine you're about to give a presentation. Your inner voice says, *"You're going to fail."* Counter this with, *"I am prepared and capable,"* and visualise a successful outcome.

Parenting Scenario: When feeling overwhelmed, instead of thinking, *"I'm a bad parent,"* remind yourself, *"Parenting is tough, but I'm doing my best."*

Relationship Scenario: Instead of dwelling on a mistake and thinking, *"I always mess up,"* try thinking, *"I made a mistake, but I can learn from it and improve."*

The Intriguing Science of Self-Talk: A Journey Through the Brain

Picture your brain as a complex orchestra, with different sections playing distinct roles in shaping your self-talk. This internal dialogue is not just a random occurrence; it's deeply rooted in your brain's neurological pathways.

Neurological Foundations: The prefrontal cortex, responsible for decision-making and social interactions, plays a significant role in self-talk. When you engage in internal dialogue, this area becomes active, influencing your choices and behaviours.

Emotional Regulation: The amygdala, our vibrant processing centre, also contributes. It colours our self-talk with emotional tones, which is why some people's self-talk may be more anxious or negative while others remain optimistic.

Memory and Self-Talk: Central to memory formation, the hippocampus links past experiences to present self-talk.

This connection explains why individuals with different life experiences have varying internal dialogues.

The fascinating diversity in people's self-talk arises from a blend of factors: Genetic Makeup, Life Experiences, Cultural Influence, etc.

> **Exercises for Transformative Self-Talk**
>
> 1. **Brain Training:** Engage in activities that challenge and stimulate your brain, such as puzzles or learning a new skill. This can positively impact the neural pathways involved in self-talk.
>
> 2. **Emotional Literacy:** Develop a deeper understanding of your emotions. Being able to identify and articulate feelings can help in reshaping negative self-talk. For this, just ask yourself as often as you can, *"what do I feel?" "Why do I feel that?"*
>
> 3. **Cultural Exploration**: Understand how your cultural background influences your self-talk. Embracing cultural diversity can enrich and balance your internal dialogue.

In addition to simple exercises, we can use one of the NLP Strategies for Positive Self-Communication, The Swish Pattern you have already met in the previous chapter.

This technique is designed to change unwanted behaviours or thoughts by swiftly swapping them with more empowering ones. This is the best technique for our current learning goal to deal with inappropriate self-talk. Here's a detailed breakdown of how to implement the Swish Pattern:

Step 1: Identify the Unwanted Behavior or Thought

› **Recognition:** Identify the specific behaviour or thought pattern you wish to change. It could be a harmful self-talk habit, such as telling yourself, *"I'm not good enough."*

- **Visualization:** Visualize a scenario where this behaviour or thought typically arises. Make this mental image as vivid as possible, including details like where you are, what you see, and how you feel.

Step 2: Choose a Replacement Image

- **Positive Image:** Select an empowering image representing the desired change or state. For example, I'd like you to envision yourself confident in completing a task you previously felt was difficult.
- **Detailing:** Make this positive image vibrant and detailed. Focus on your looks, emotions, and sense of accomplishment.

Step 3: The Swish Technique

- **Superimposition:** In your mind, place the negative image in the foreground and the positive image in the background, as if the positive image is far away.
- **Swishing:** Now, quickly 'swish' the two images so the positive image rapidly comes to the forefront, growing more extensive and precise, while the negative image recedes and diminishes.
- **Sound Effect:** Optionally, you can add a 'swishing' sound effect in your mind to enhance the effect.

Step 4: Repeat and Reinforce

- **Repetition:** Repeat the swish several times, making the transition more decisive.
- **Reinforcement:** After each swish, take a moment to bask in the positive emotions associated with the new image.

Step 5: Test and Evaluate

- **Testing:** Think about the original situation or behaviour. Have your response or feelings towards it changed?

Internal Dialogue and Self-Talk

> **Adjustment:** If the unwanted thought or behaviour still arises, repeat the process, adjusting the images or the speed of the swish as needed.

The Swish Pattern is a powerful NLP technique that leverages the brain's visual and associative powers to alter habitual thought patterns. Repeating negative thoughts with positive, empowering images can reprogram your mind to engage in more positive self-communication. Like many NLP strategies, this technique is highly individualised, so feel free to adapt it to suit your imagery and experiences better.

6.3 Dissolving Negative Self-Talk Patterns

To dissolve Negative self-talk in these patterns, it's crucial to implement strategies that can rewire our thought processes. Here are some fundamental approaches:

1. Mindfulness and Self-Awareness

Awareness: The first step is to become aware of your negative self-talk. Mindfulness practices can help you recognise when you are engaging in negative self-talk.

Observation: Instead of engaging with these thoughts, observe them as outsiders. This detachment can reduce their power over you.

2. Challenging Negative Thoughts

Questioning: Actively challenge your negative thoughts. Ask yourself whether they are indeed accurate or if you're exaggerating the negativity.

Evidence-Based Thinking: Look for evidence that contradicts your negative thoughts. This can help in reevaluating their validity.

3. Cognitive Restructuring

Reframing: Cognitive restructuring involves reframing negative thoughts into more positive, realistic ones. For instance, instead of thinking, *"I always fail,"* reframe it to, *"I've had some setbacks, but I also have successes."*

Positive Affirmations: Regularly using positive affirmations can help to counterbalance negative self-talk.

4. Emotional Regulation Techniques

Breathing Exercises: Techniques such as deep breathing can help calm the mind, making it easier to manage negative thoughts.

Emotional Release: Activities like journaling or talking to a trusted person can provide an outlet for the emotions driving negative self-talk.

5. Behavioral Changes

Action-Oriented Approach: Taking small, manageable actions towards your goals can build confidence and reduce negative self-talk.

Habitual Changes: Changing your routine or environment can disrupt negative thought patterns.

6. Professional Help

Therapy: Sometimes, working with a therapist or counsellor can be essential in overcoming deeply ingrained negative self-talk patterns.

Cognitive Behavioral Therapy (CBT): CBT is particularly effective in addressing negative self-talk, focusing on changing thought patterns to improve mental health.

7. Building a Support Network

Seeking Support: Surrounding yourself with positive, supportive people can influence your thought patterns.

Community Engagement: Engaging in community activities or support groups can provide encouragement and alternative perspectives.

8. Continuous Learning and Personal Development

Reading and Education: Educate yourself on personal development and mental health to gain tools and insights.

Workshops and Seminars: Participating in workshops and seminars can provide new strategies and a sense of shared experience.

Dissolving negative self-talk patterns requires a multifaceted approach. It involves becoming aware of and challenging these thoughts, using cognitive and emotional tools to reshape them, making behavioural changes, seeking professional help when necessary, and continuously learning and growing. Over time, these strategies can significantly shift how you talk to yourself, paving the way for a more positive and fulfilling life.

Chapter 7:
NLP in Personal Relationships

7.1 Is it fair?

The main thing to consider when using NLP in personal relationships is why and how you use it. If you're using NLP techniques because you want to understand your partner better, communicate more clearly, or resolve conflicts in a healthier way, that's generally a good thing. It's about improving the relationship for both of you, ensuring you feel heard and understood.

But, and this is a big but, if the intention is to manipulate or control the other person, that's not fair at all. Relationships are built on trust and respect, and using any psychological technique to manipulate someone breaks that trust. It's really about the golden rule. Treat others the way you want to be treated. If you wouldn't want someone using these techniques to manipulate you, then it's unfair to do it to them.

Also, it's essential to be open and honest in a relationship. If you're using NLP techniques, it's better to be upfront about it. Transparency is key. You don't need to make a big announcement or anything, but incorporate these techniques respectfully and openly. Your partner may want to learn more about this introductory psychology, and you both can practise helping each other and looking in one direction.

Remember, in any relationship, it's more about working on yourself than trying to change the other person. So, if you're using NLP to become a better listener, to manage your emotions better, or to communicate more effectively, that's great. That's about you growing and contributing positively to the relationship.

So, using NLP in personal relationships can be okay, even beneficial, as long as it's done with the right intentions and in a respectful, transparent way. It's all about improving the relationship and ensuring both feel valued and understood, not gaining the upper hand or manipulating the other person.

7.2 Rapport Building, Mirroring and Matching Techniques

Rapport Building: The Key to Connection

In the realm of personal relationships, establishing rapport is fundamental. Rapport is a harmonious connection where both parties feel understood, valued, and respected. It's the foundation upon which solid and meaningful relationships are built.

> **Theoretical Basis:**
>
> Rapport building in NLP is rooted in the understanding that people are more receptive and responsive to those similar to them in some way.
>
> This connection isn't just about shared interests or beliefs; it's also about synchronising subconsciously through body language, tonality, and even breathing patterns.

Mirroring and Matching Techniques

Mirroring and matching are practical techniques used in NLP to establish and deepen rapport. These techniques involve subtly matching or mirroring another person's body language, vocal qualities, or breathing patterns.

Mirroring: This involves replicating the body language of the other person. If they lean forward, you lean forward. If they gesture with their hands while talking, you incorporate similar gestures. It's like a subtle dance where you reflect their physical movements.

Matching: This technique is slightly more nuanced than mirroring. Instead of directly copying movements, you adopt similar postures or gestures. For example, if someone speaks softly, you lower your voice to match their tone.

> **Theoretical Basis:**
>
> The principle behind these techniques is that they create a subconscious sense of familiarity and agreement, fostering a deeper level of connection and understanding.
>
> When it comes to rapport building, mirroring, and matching techniques in NLP, the stage of the relationship – it's just starting or has been going on for years – changes how these techniques are used and why.

In a new relationship, these techniques are often about establishing a connection and getting to know each other better. When you're just starting, you're both figuring out if you're a good match, right? So, mirroring and matching – like adopting similar body language or matching the tone of voice – can help create a sense of comfort and connection. It's like speaking the same emotional language, which can be important when building trust and understanding in those early stages.

On the other hand, in a long-term relationship, it's a bit different. You already know each other pretty well, and there's a level of comfort and familiarity there. Here, rapport building and mirroring are more about maintaining and deepening the connection you already have. It's less about trying to establish a bond and more about reinforcing and nurturing the bond that's already there.

These techniques can also help smooth rough patches or misunderstandings in long-term relationships. If you've been together for years and hit a communication snag, consciously mirroring your partner's body language or speech patterns can help remind you of your deeper connection. It's like a subtle way of saying, *"I'm still with you; I still get you,"* even if you're going through a tough time.

So, for new relationships, rapport building and mirroring are about establishing that initial connection and finding common ground. Long-term relationships are more about maintaining and deepening the connection and reminding each other of the bond you share, especially when things get challenging.

Let's look at practical exercises tailored for new and long-term relationships, focusing on rapport-building, mirroring, and matching techniques.

For New Relationships:

1. Active Listening Exercise:

Purpose: *To build a deeper understanding of the early stages of a relationship.*

How to Do It: Focus entirely on what your partner says in your conversations. Listen without planning your response. After they finish speaking, summarise what they said to show that you've genuinely listened and understood.

2. Matching Moods:

Purpose: *To create a sense of empathy and connection.*

How to Do It: Pay attention to your partner's mood and energy level. If they're excited, match that enthusiasm in your response. If they're more subdued, adopt a calmer demeanour. This helps in creating a sense of emotional alignment.

1. Shared Experiences Activity:

Purpose: *To find common ground and interests.*

How to Do It: Plan activities that both of you are interested in or curious about. Please discuss your experiences afterwards, focusing on what you both enjoyed and learned.

For Long-Term Relationships:

1. Mirroring Exercise:

Purpose: *To re-establish connection and empathy.*

How to Do It: Choose a relaxed setting. Sit facing each other and take turns mirroring each other's body language. This can include posture, gestures, or facial expressions. It should be done subtly and respectfully.

2. Memory Lane:

Purpose: *To reignite shared memories and strengthen bonds.*

How to Do It: Spend time together reminiscing about your early days as a couple. Look at old photos or visit places that are significant to your relationship. Share what those memories mean to each of you.

3. Communication Role-Play:

Purpose: *To enhance understanding and communication.*

How to Do It: Take turns discussing a topic from the other person's perspective. This helps understand each other's viewpoints and feelings, especially on issues with differing opinions.

Everyday Tips for Both:

- **Consistent Check-ins:** Regularly discuss your feelings and experiences in the relationship. This helps in maintaining open lines of communication.

- **Empathy Building:** Regularly express what you appreciate about each other. This fosters a positive and supportive environment.

- **Mindfulness in Interaction:** Be mindful of your tone of voice and non-verbal cues during interactions. They can have a significant impact on how your communication is perceived.

Remember, the key to these exercises is genuine effort and a desire to understand and connect with your partner. Whether you're just starting or have been together for years, these practices can help nurture a healthy and fulfilling relationship.

7.3 Conflict Resolution through NLP

Conflict in relationships is inevitable, but NLP offers tools to navigate and resolve these conflicts more effectively.

Technique: Reframing in Conflict
Reframing in NLP involves changing the perspective on a conflict situation to find a more positive or constructive outlook.

By reframing, you can shift from a blame-focused perspective to one that seeks understanding and solutions.

Technique: Effective Communication Strategies
NLP emphasises the importance of clear and empathetic communication.

Techniques such as active listening, sensory-based language, and expressing oneself clearly and respectfully are crucial in resolving conflicts.

Technique: Outcome-Based Thinking
This involves focusing on the desired outcome of a conflict resolution process rather than getting bogged down by the details of the disagreement.

By keeping the end goal in sight, it becomes easier to navigate through the conflict and work towards a mutually beneficial resolution.

Here are a couple of examples that illustrate how NLP techniques can be applied:

> **Example 1: Reframing a Conflict**
>
> **Situation:** *Imagine a couple, Alex and Jordan, who have a recurring conflict about household chores. Alex feels they are taking on more than their fair share of the chores, leading to resentment.*
>
> **NLP Technique:** Reframing the Situation

Application:

Step 1: Alex is encouraged to express their feelings without blame, focusing on their emotions rather than Jordan's actions.

Step 2: Together, they explore different ways to view the situation. For example, instead of seeing the imbalance as a sign of disrespect, they might reframe it as a misunderstanding of each other's expectations.

Step 3: This reframing helps to depersonalise the conflict and opens up a conversation about how both partners can contribute to a fairer distribution of chores.

Example 2: Anchoring in Heated Moments

Situation: *In another scenario, Sam and Riley often have their discussions escalating into heated arguments, making it hard to resolve conflicts constructively.*

NLP Technique: Anchoring for Emotional Regulation

Application:

Step 1: Sam and Riley each identify a physical action (e.g., touching a necklace or pressing a finger against the palm) that they associate with feelings of calm and understanding.

Step 2: They practice this anchoring in moments of calm, linking the action to feelings of love and understanding for each other.

Step 3: When a conflict starts to heat up, they use their anchors to help regain emotional control and constructively approach the situation.

Example 3: The Meta-Model for Clarification

Situation: *Chris and Taylor often speak too emotionally during conflicts, leading to unnecessary misunderstandings.*

NLP Technique: Using the Meta-Model for Clear Communication

Application:

- **Step 1:** When a misunderstanding arises, they use Meta-Model questions to clarify each other's statements. For example, if Taylor says, "You never listen to me," Chris might ask, "When you say 'never,' can you give me a specific example?"

- **Step 2:** This approach helps break down generalisations and assumptions, allowing for a clearer understanding of each other's perspectives.

General Principles in NLP Conflict Resolution:

Active Listening: Ensuring each partner feels heard and understood.

Empathy and Understanding: Trying to see the situation from the other person's perspective.

Collaborative Problem-Solving: Working together to find mutually beneficial solutions.

Using these NLP techniques in personal relationships can help transform conflicts from destructive to constructive, fostering better understanding and stronger connections.

Chapter 8: Romantic Relationships and NLP

Welcome to a pivotal chapter in your journey through NLP, where we delve into romance. Have you ever wondered how some couples maintain a spark that seems to defy time? Or how they navigate conflicts with grace and emerge stronger? This chapter is your gateway to understanding and applying NLP in a way that can significantly elevate your romantic relationship. It's not just about avoiding misunderstandings or resolving conflicts; it's about enriching the very fabric of your connection. Prepare to discover insights and techniques that could transform 'just getting along' into a deeper, more intuitive understanding and bond with your partner. Let's turn the page to a chapter of love, understanding, and profound connection.

8.1 Deepening Intimacy with Meta Programs

Various psychological approaches, including NLP, can enhance and deepen romantic relationships, focusing on improving communication, resolving conflicts, and enriching intimacy, including using Meta Programs for deepening intimacy, which I will describe in this chapter.

The most significant approaches and scientists or directions of psychology may be seen below:

Communication and Understanding

1. **Active Listening** (Counseling Psychology):
   Active listening involves fully concentrating, understanding, responding, and remembering what is being said. In

relationships, making your partner feel heard and understood is crucial.

2. **The Five Love Languages** (Gary Chapman):
Understanding your partner's love language (Words of Affirmation, Acts of Service, Receiving Gifts, Quality Time, Physical Touch) can profoundly improve how you express love and care.

3. **NLP Mirroring and Matching:**
These techniques can create a sense of empathy and connection. Mirroring your partner's gestures, tone of voice, or breathing patterns can enhance rapport and emotional connection.

Conflict Resolution

1. **The Gottman Method** (John Gottman):
Gottman's research emphasises managing conflict rather than avoiding it. Techniques include softening startup (how you initiate a conversation), making repair attempts (signals to de-escalate arguments), and seeking to understand before being understood.

2. **NLP Reframing:**
Viewing conflicts from different perspectives can often defuse tension. Reframing challenges as opportunities for growth can change the dynamics of a conflict.

Deepening Intimacy with Meta Programs

1. **Understanding Meta Programs:**
Meta Programs in NLP are internal processes that guide how we make sense of the world. In relationships, understanding your and your partner's meta-programs can deepen intimacy. For example, recognising these differences can enhance understanding and patience if one person is more 'towards' motivated (motivated by goals and achievements) and the other is more 'away from' (motivated by avoiding problems).

2. **Adjusting Communication Styles:**
   Adapting your communication to align with your partner's Meta Programs can improve your connection. For example, if your partner focuses on details (specific), use more detailed communication instead of big-picture (global) talk.

3. **Aligning Life Goals:**
   Understanding each other's Meta Programs can help align life goals and values, making it easier to make decisions that satisfy both partners.

Maintaining a Healthy Relationship

1. **Emotionally Focused Therapy** (Sue Johnson):
   This approach focuses on creating and strengthening the emotional bond between partners, emphasising emotional responsiveness and attachment needs.

2. **Regular Check-Ins and Appreciation:**
   Regularly discussing each other's needs and showing appreciation can strengthen the relationship. Simple gestures of gratitude and acknowledgement can go a long way.

3. **Mindfulness and Presence:**
   Being fully present with your partner, without distractions, can significantly improve the quality of your interactions.

Exercise 1: The Love Language Exchange

Objective: To understand and appreciate each other's love languages (inspired by Gary Chapman's Five Love Languages).

STEPS:

1. **Identify Your Love Languages:** Each partner takes a turn to identify and share their primary love language (Words of Affirmation, Acts of Service, Receiving Gifts, Quality Time, Physical Touch). Then, explain specific actions or words that make you feel loved in that language to your partner.

2. **Plan a Love Language Day:** Dedicate a day where each partner focuses on expressing love in the other's primary love language. For example, if your partner's love language is 'Quality Time,' you plan a day of shared activities you enjoy.
3. **Reflect and Share:** At the end of the day, discuss how you each felt about the experience. Were there any surprises? Did specific actions make you feel particularly loved or appreciated?

> **Exercise 2:** The Meta Program Connection
>
> **Objective:** To understand each other's Meta Programs and how they influence communication and decision-making.

STEPS:

1. **Learn About Meta Programs:** Research and learn about Meta Programs, such as 'towards vs away from' motivation, 'big picture vs. detail-oriented,' 'options vs. procedures,' etc.
2. **Identify Personal Meta Programs:** Each partner takes time to reflect on their dominant Meta Programs. Could you share these, providing examples of how they manifest in your behaviours and decision-making?
3. **Role Reversal Activity:** Engage in a role reversal where each partner tries to see a situation or decide from the other's Meta Program perspective. For example, if one is 'big picture' and the other is 'detail-oriented,' each tries to approach a situation from the other's perspective.
4. **Discussion and Reflection:** Discuss how this role reversal felt. Was it challenging to think differently? Did it change your understanding of your partner's reactions and decisions?

These exercises are designed to foster deeper understanding and empathy in a relationship. By actively engaging in these activities, partners can gain insights into each other's emotional needs and thought processes, leading to a more harmonious and connected relationship.

8.2 The Love Strategies: Understanding Partners' Needs

Love strategies in a relationship? Every one of us has a unique way of feeling loved and appreciated. It's like having a secret recipe for happiness, but sometimes we forget to share it with our partners. And let's be honest, they're not mind readers (as much as we wish they were).

Use NLP's insights to tune into each other's emotional frequencies!

First up, let's talk about 'calibration.' In NLP, this means being super observant. Pay attention to the small changes in your partner's mood and behaviour. Did their smile reach their eyes when you surprised them with breakfast in bed? That's a clue! Calibration helps you understand what makes your partner feel loved and valued.

Then, there's 'mirroring.' Mirroring subtly matches their body language, tone of voice, or breathing patterns. It's a way of saying, *"I'm with you,"* without words. When done right, it creates a dance where you both feel more connected and in sync.

Remember the power of 'anchoring.' Remember that time you both laughed till your bellies hurt? Anchor that feeling. Maybe it's a unique word or a gentle touch on the arm. Later, using that anchor can bring back those good vibes when the seas get choppy.

Tony Robbins talks a lot about understanding each other's 'world.' It's about genuinely getting where your partner is coming from, their beliefs, their values, and the weird quirks that make them, well, them. It's about celebrating these differences, not just tolerating them.

It helps navigate the beautiful, sometimes messy, but always rewarding journey of understanding your partner's needs and love strategies. Keep it fun, keep it accurate, and who knows? You might find the treasure of a lifetime – a deeper, more fulfilling relationship.

8.3 NLP for Healing and Growth in Relationships

Meet Sarah and Alex, a couple who, like many, have encountered their share of challenges in their romantic journey. Despite their deep love for each other, they've struggled with miscommunication, misunderstandings, and typical conflicts in long-term relationships. These difficulties have often led to frustration and emotional distance, making them question how to navigate these turbulent waters and find a path to a stronger, more fulfilling partnership. In this context, they turn to advanced NLP techniques and psychological insights, seeking tools and strategies to overcome these hurdles and foster more profound understanding, communication, and emotional connection.

In exploring the nuanced world of romantic relationships through the lens of NLP and psychology, we uncover a realm where communication and emotional understanding are paramount. The journey begins with the NLP Meta-Model, a powerful tool that helps couples like Sarah and Alex dissect and understand their communication patterns. By adopting Meta-Model questions, they learn to unravel the complexities of their conversations, leading to more prosperous, more empathetic exchanges. This approach doesn't just clear up misunderstandings; it deepens their connection, making each conversation a step towards greater intimacy.

However, the challenges of a relationship aren't confined to communication alone. Conflict is an inevitable guest in the journey of two intertwined lives. Here, the technique of reframing in NLP becomes invaluable. Sarah and Alex learn to see conflicts not as threats but as opportunities for mutual growth. They begin to understand each other's perspectives, transforming potential arguments into moments of understanding. Reframing their conflicts, they plant seeds for a more resilient and understanding relationship.

Another transformative aspect of NLP in their relationship is the use of anchoring. During moments of joy and closeness, they create positive emotional anchors. These anchors are potent tools during distress, helping them return to mutual understanding and love. The ability to anchor positive emotions and recall them in challenging times becomes a cornerstone in their journey towards a harmonious relationship.

Integrating psychological concepts like Attachment Theory, Sarah and Alex gain insights into their behaviours and needs. Understanding their attachment styles sheds light on the deeper reasons behind their actions and reactions within the relationship. This knowledge empowers them to tailor their communication and responses, fostering a more secure and nurturing bond.

Incorporating Emotionally Focused Therapy (EFT) elements, they adopt practices like mirroring to ensure they hear and genuinely understand each other. This deep level of empathy, achieved through the reflective listening encouraged by EFT, helps them navigate emotional complexities with more excellent care and understanding.

Integrating Mindfulness-Based Stress Reduction (MBSR) techniques brings a new dimension of emotional regulation and presence into their relationship. Through mindfulness, they learn to respond thoughtfully to each other's needs and emotions, cultivating a relationship environment where each moment and feeling is acknowledged and valued.

By continuously developing their emotional intelligence, Sarah and Alex enhance their capacity for empathy and understanding. They become more attuned to each other's emotional states, leading to a relationship characterised by deep emotional connection and mutual respect.

In the spirit of Narrative Therapy, they begin to reshape their relationship story, focusing on their journey's strengths and positive experiences. Reframing their shared narrative celebrates their past and paves the way for a future filled with hope and mutual growth.

Adopting principles from the Gottman Method, such as building love maps and nurturing their emotional connection, strengthens their relationship's foundation. They learn to turn towards each other's needs and desires, creating a relationship that thrives on understanding, respect, and continuous growth.

The growth experienced within a romantic relationship often has a profound ripple effect, extending far beyond the confines of the partnership itself. When individuals understand, empathise, and effectively communicate with their partners, they inadvertently cultivate invaluable skills in other areas of life. This growth is not just emotional but also psychological and interpersonal. For instance, patience and active listening honed in a relationship can translate into better team collaboration in a professional setting. The ability to manage and express emotions effectively, a skill sharpened within the dynamics of a partnership, can lead to more resilient and adaptive coping strategies in personal challenges.

Moreover, the confidence and self-awareness gained through a healthy relationship often empower individuals to pursue personal goals and aspirations with greater vigour and clarity. This is because successfully navigating relationship complexities builds a foundational sense of self-efficacy and problem-solving skills applicable in varied life scenarios. Therefore, the personal development achieved through romantic relationships catalyses overall growth, impacting career success, social interactions, and even personal aspirations. It highlights an essential truth: the quality of our relationships often mirrors and influences the quality of our lives.

Chapter 9: NLP in the Workplace

In the fast-paced and dynamic environment of the modern workplace, Neuro-Linguistic Programming (NLP) emerges as a vital toolkit. This chapter delves into how NLP can be harnessed to enhance communication, negotiation, and leadership, focusing on negotiation and persuasion techniques.

9.1 Effective Communication Strategies

Effective communication in the workplace goes beyond mere exchange of information; it's about understanding the underlying emotions, intentions, and thoughts of others. NLP offers a unique approach to achieve this that we have already explored for other life cases.

Rapport Building: A foundational element of NLP, rapport building involves mirroring body language, tone of voice, and speech patterns to create a sense of familiarity and trust. For instance, a manager might subtly adopt a team member's posture or speech tempo during one-on-one meetings to foster a more open and comfortable communication environment.

Meta-Model Questions: Using targeted questions to uncover the specific details and structure of a colleague's thought process can clarify vague statements and assumptions, leading to more precise and meaningful conversations.

Imagine a scenario where Emma, a team leader, prepares for a crucial team meeting. She aims to discuss upcoming project changes, which she knows might be met with resistance. To ensure effective communication, Emma decided to utilise NLP rapport-building techniques.

As the meeting begins, Emma consciously mirrors her team members' body language and speech patterns. When she notices that one of her team members, John, is speaking in a measured, thoughtful manner, she adjusts her speech to match his tempo and style. Similarly, when interacting with Lisa, who uses more expressive gestures, Emma subtly incorporates similar gestures into her conversation.

By mirroring these verbal and non-verbal cues, Emma creates a sense of familiarity and trust within the team. This approach makes her team members feel more understood and valued and opens them up to be more receptive to the changes she proposes. The meeting proceeds with more openness and collaboration, paving the way for a more productive and positive discussion.

9.2 Negotiation and Persuasion Techniques

NLP shines in Negotiation and persuasion, offering nuanced strategies beyond traditional approaches.

Calibration: This involves reading subtle cues in body language and speech patterns to gauge a person's true feelings or reactions. For example, a skilled negotiator might notice a slight hesitation or change in voice pitch, indicating a point of resistance or concern, and address it directly to move the negotiation forward.

Advanced Reframing: In negotiation, reframing involves presenting information or a proposal that aligns with the listener's values and beliefs. Imagine a salesperson reframing a product's cost as an investment in long-term savings and efficiency for a cost-conscious client.

Anchoring in Negotiations: Anchors can be set up during positive moments in a negotiation and activated later to recall those positive emotions. For instance, a negotiator might use a specific gesture or word during a moment of agreement, which can later be used to bring the discussion back to a positive focus when encountering resistance.

Sleight of Mouth Patterns: These are verbal patterns used to redirect someone's thought process. In a negotiation, if a client says, *"This solution is too expensive,"* a response using Sleight of Mouth might be, "How can we afford not to invest in a solution that brings long-term benefits?"

9.3 Leadership and Team-Building through NLP

Leadership and team-building are enhanced through applying NLP by fostering a deeper understanding of team dynamics and individual motivations.

Modelling Excellence: NLP encourages leaders to model behaviours of excellence. For instance, a leader might adopt the conflict resolution skills of a respected mentor, applying these strategies within their team to enhance cohesion.

Empowering Language Patterns: Leaders can use language that empowers and motivates, turning challenges into opportunities for growth and learning within the team.

Consider a scenario where Michael, a department manager, faces challenges with frequent conflicts within his team. These conflicts are impacting team morale and productivity. To address this, Michael recalls a former mentor, Susan, who was exceptionally skilled at managing team disputes. He begins to analyse Susan's approach: her calm demeanour, active listening to all parties, and ability to reframe problems into solutions. Michael realised that Susan often used empathetic language and sought to understand the underlying concerns of each team member rather than just addressing surface issues.

Michael starts by changing his approach to conflicts to implement this in his team. In the next team meeting, he remains calm and composed when a disagreement arises, mirroring Susan's demeanour. He listens intently to each team member's perspective, validating their feelings and concerns. Michael then skillfully reframes the problem, guiding the team to see it as a shared challenge that requires a collaborative solution.

By modelling Susan's conflict resolution skills, Michael resolves the immediate disagreement and sets a new standard for handling conflicts within his team. Over time, the team members emulate these behaviours, leading to a more harmonious and collaborative working environment. This example demonstrates how NLP's 'Modeling Excellence' technique can be effectively applied in a leadership context to build stronger, more cohesive teams.

Chapter 10: Advanced Communication Techniques

In professional and personal growth, mastering advanced communication techniques is crucial. This chapter delves into three sophisticated approaches: The Milton Model, Meta Programs, and the use of Presuppositions, each offering unique insights and applications for enhancing influence and understanding in various interactions.

10.1 The Milton Model: Persuasive Language Patterns

The Milton Model, named after Milton Erickson, a renowned psychiatrist and psychologist, is a cornerstone of NLP that focuses on using persuasive and hypnotic language patterns. This model employs artfully vague and metaphorical language, allowing the listener to fill in the gaps with their own experiences and interpretations, leading to greater acceptance and influence.

> **Example:** A manager aiming to motivate her team might say, *"Imagine a future where our project not only meets but exceeds our expectations, bringing success in ways we might not yet fully realise."* This statement, while vague, opens up a space for team members to envision success in a way that resonates personally with them, thereby increasing their motivation and commitment.

10.2 Meta Programs: Understanding People's Motivations

Meta Programs are internal processes that act as filters for our experiences, influencing how we process information and make decisions. Understanding these can help tailor communication to align with individuals' intrinsic motivations.

> **Example:** If a team member is motivated by 'towards' goals (seeking to achieve specific outcomes) rather than 'away from' goals (looking to avoid adverse outcomes), a leader can frame tasks and objectives in a positive, goal-oriented manner, such as, *"Completing this project will lead us to new opportunities and recognition,"* instead of emphasising the avoidance of failure.

10.3 Utilising Presuppositions for Influence

Presuppositions are assumptions implicit in our language that can be used to influence thought and behaviour subtly. One can gently guide the listener's thought process by embedding presuppositions in communication.

Advanced Communication Techniques

> **Example:** In a negotiation, a business leader might say, *"When you've realised the long-term benefits of our partnership, what would be the first step you'd like to take?"* This sentence presupposes that the listener will see the benefits, subtly steering the conversation towards planning future actions rather than debating the partnership's value.

These advanced communication techniques offer powerful tools for professionals seeking to enhance their influence, persuasion, and understanding of others. The Milton Model, with its hypnotic language patterns, is invaluable for creating persuasive narratives. Meta Programs provide deep insights into individual motivations, enabling tailored communication strategies. Lastly, the strategic use of Presuppositions can subtly influence thinking and decision-making. Together, these techniques form a sophisticated toolkit for anyone looking to elevate their communication skills to an advanced level.

PART 3
Self-Transformation and Achieving Goals through NLP

Chapter 11: Goal Setting with NLP

11.1 The Evolution of SMART Goals: An NLP Enhanced Approach

The SMART model is a time-tested framework, but NLP takes it further, infusing it with sensory and emotional dimensions to make goals more vivid and compelling.

> **Example:** Instead of setting a goal as *"I will increase my professional network by 30% in six months,"* an NLP-enhanced approach would be to visualise specific interactions, feel the excitement of new connections, and hear the conversations of a growing network. This sensory-rich goal setting makes the objective more tangible and engaging.

11.2 The Well-Formed Outcome: A Blueprint for Success

The Well-Formed Outcome: Crafting Comprehensive Goals

The Well-Formed Outcome is a quintessential NLP technique that provides a holistic blueprint for goal setting, ensuring that goals are congruent with personal values and life contexts.

> **Practical Exercise:** Ask, *"What specifically do I want to achieve?"* Then, delve deeper with questions like, *"How will achieving this goal affect my life?"* and *"What resources do I need?"* This comprehensive questioning leads to a well-rounded and profoundly integrated goal.

11.3 Overcoming Obstacles and Maintaining Motivation

In the journey towards goal achievement, obstacles are inevitable, but they don't have to derail progress. Fear stops actions; actions stop fear.

Logical Levels of Change: This NLP strategy involves addressing obstacles by examining them across different logical levels: environment, behaviour, capabilities, beliefs and values, identity, and purpose. For instance, when encountering a challenge, could you assess how it impacts each level? This comprehensive analysis can reveal hidden solutions and provide a multi-dimensional approach to overcoming obstacles. For example, if a professional struggles with a challenging project (behaviour level), they might reassess their beliefs about their capabilities or even consider how this project aligns with their broader purpose. This layered approach often leads to more innovative and sustainable solutions.

Pattern Interrupt: Break the cycle of negative thinking that often accompanies obstacles. When stuck in a loop of unproductive thoughts, engage in an activity that disrupts this pattern, such as a physical exercise or a creative task. This reset can shift your mental state and open up new perspectives.

Ecology Check for Goal Alignment: Conduct an 'ecology check' to ensure your pursuit aligns with all aspects of your life. I'd like you to reflect on how the goal and its obstacles resonate with your broader values and life context. This can provide insights into the nature of the obstacle and pathways to overcome it.

Creating a Compelling Future Vision: Develop a vivid and compelling vision of your life after overcoming the current challenges. This vision should be holistic, encompassing the achievement and the overall enhancement of life quality. It serves as a powerful motivator, especially when faced with daunting obstacles.

Employing NLP strategies like the Logical Levels of Change provides a multi-faceted approach to overcoming obstacles. By understanding challenges at different levels – from behaviour to purpose – we gain a deeper insight into their nature and potential solutions. This, along with pattern interruptions, ecology checks, and future visioning, equips us with a robust toolkit for navigating hurdles, aligning our goals with our broader life context, and moving forward with resilience and clarity.

Chapter 12: Transforming Habits with NLP

12.1 Identifying and Changing Limiting Habits

Understanding and transforming habits is a multi-faceted process involving insights from psychology, neuroscience, and practical strategies for change.

Formation and Types of Habits:

1. **Passive and Active Habits:** French philosopher Bergson distinguished between passive habits, which develop from repeated exposure, and active habits, formed through intentional effort. Passive habits arise naturally, like adapting to a high altitude, whereas active habits are akin to skill development, such as a gymnast mastering routines.

2. **Neuroscientific Perspective:** The neuroscience of habit formation points to the basal ganglia, an ancient brain region that significantly coordinates voluntary movements and habit formation. Initially, conscious and goal-directed actions, through repetition, become automatic habits embedded in our brain circuitry. Habits form through an interplay of associative

and automatic pathways in the basal ganglia, with positive reinforcement, often triggered by dopamine release, being a crucial aspect.

3. **Behavioral Theories:** William James and B.F. Skinner contributed significantly to habit theory. James viewed habit as the ingraining of repeated actions, while Skinner emphasised the role of rewards in habit formation. Skinner's experiments demonstrated that behaviours engaged for rewards tend to become habits.

Transforming Limiting Habits:

1. **Reducing Stress:** Many negative habits are responses to stress. Techniques like yogic breathing, mindfulness, and simple physical activities can help lower stress levels, making it easier to break these habits.

2. **Awareness of Negative Habits:** Since habits are often automatic, becoming mindful of them and the experiences they involve can facilitate breaking them. For example, smokers who become aware of the actual sensations of smoking often find it easier to quit.

3. **Replacing Old Habits:** Replacing a harmful habit with a positive one that opposes it can be effective. This involves planning a different course of action and repeatedly engaging in it, as demonstrated in studies of workplace recycling habits.

Psychological Approaches to Changing Limiting Beliefs:

1. **Rational Emotive Behavior Therapy (REBT):** REBT helps identify negative or irrational thought patterns that affect behaviour. It employs the ABC model to trace and challenge self-limiting beliefs. For example, understanding how an activating event leads to a belief, resulting in a consequence, can help reframe thoughts and responses.

2. **Cognitive Restructuring:** This technique, part of cognitive-behavioural therapy (CBT), involves challenging cognitive distortions. Socratic questioning, a method of cognitive

restructuring, asks focused questions to challenge black-and-white thinking and ensure thoughts are based on sound logic.

3. **Schema Therapy:** Schema therapy can be beneficial for more profound, more ingrained self-limiting beliefs. It addresses early maladaptive schemas that develop during childhood and influence self-esteem and self-image. Techniques in schema therapy include empathic confrontation and limited re-parents.

The most desired life-improving habits that people around the world strive for:

1. **Health:** Aiming for 10,000 steps daily can support other positive health habits.

2. **Finance:** Journaling expenses encourage financial awareness and planning.

3. **Career:** Active goal setting and effective time management using the Eisenhower quadrant system can be transformative.

4. **Wellness:** Daily gratitude practice can shift focus from lack to appreciation and abundance.

12.2 Installing New, Empowering Habits

Installing new, empowering habits is a process that involves awareness, planning, and consistent effort. Here are some practical steps and techniques for creating and maintaining new habits:

1. **Build Awareness:** Begin by noticing your current habits and identifying one you wish to change. Making a list of your daily routines can be helpful in recognising patterns and areas for improvement.

2. **Habit Stacking:** Attach a new habit to something you already do regularly. For instance, if you want to start walking daily, do it right after a routine activity like lunch. This method,

known as habit stacking, links a new habit with an established one, making it easier to remember and perform.

3. **Start with Small Habits:** Choose a new habit that is simple enough to accomplish without requiring significant motivation. Starting with a highly manageable step ensures the habit is easy to adopt. For example, if your goal is to exercise more, start with just two minutes of exercise per day.

4. **Gradual Improvement:** Make tiny, incremental improvements. This method helps in building up the habit over time without overwhelming yourself. For example, if you start meditating for one minute daily, you could gradually increase the duration as you get more comfortable with the practice.

5. **Break Habits into Chunks:** As you build up the habit, break it into smaller, more manageable segments. This can help maintain momentum and make the habit more straightforward. For instance, if you want to meditate for 20 minutes, start with two 10-minute segments.

6. **Quick Recovery from Slip-ups:** Understand that making mistakes or missing your habit occasionally is normal. The key is to get back on track as soon as possible without being too hard on yourself. Planning and knowing how to deal with potential failures can help maintain consistency.

7. **Patience and Sustainable Pace:** Be patient and stick to a pace that you can sustain. If a habit becomes too challenging too quickly, it might become more annoying. Start with what feels easy and increase the difficulty gradually.

8. **Make it Obvious and Attractive:** Create cues in your environment to remind you of your new habit, and try to make the habit enjoyable. This can increase your likelihood of sticking with it.

9. **Make it Easy and Satisfying:** Simplify your new habit as much as possible and find ways to reward yourself for sticking to it. Rewards can reinforce the habit and make it more appealing.

10. **Consistency Over Perfection:** Focus on being consistent rather than perfect. Missing your habit once or twice isn't as important as consistently returning to it. This approach helps in building a robust and sustainable habit over time.

By following these steps and being mindful of the changes you are trying to implement, you can effectively install new, empowering habits that contribute to your personal growth and well-being.

12.3 The Role of Ecology in Habit Change

In Neuro-Linguistic Programming (NLP), "ecology" refers to considering how changes or actions fit into a person's life. It involves evaluating the impact of any change on all aspects of an individual's life and ensuring that the change is congruent with their values, beliefs, and long-term objectives.

The ecological check is a crucial step when applying NLP concepts to habit change. It asks questions like:

- How will this new habit affect different areas of my life?
- Is this habit in alignment with my values and beliefs?
- What are the potential positive and negative impacts of adopting this new habit?

The purpose of this ecological check is to ensure that the new habit is beneficial in one aspect and harmonious with the individual's overall life. This approach helps maintain a balance and avoid conflicts that might arise due to a change that is beneficial in one aspect but detrimental in another. This holistic view is essential in NLP as it ensures that changes lead to a positive overall outcome for the individual.

The ecological check in NLP is more than just a preventative measure against adverse outcomes; it is also a tool for enhancing positive change. Ensuring that a new habit aligns with multiple faces of one's life increases the likelihood that the habit will be sustainable and beneficial in the long run. This approach encourages individuals to consider the broader implications of their actions, leading to more thoughtful and meaningful habit changes.

In NLP, ecology also extends to relationships and interactions with others. When changing a habit, it's essential to consider how it might affect those around you. A new habit should not only be beneficial for the individual but should also contribute positively to their relationships and social environment.

Overall, the role of ecology in habit change within the framework of NLP emphasises a comprehensive and balanced approach to personal development. It underscores the importance of considering the broader implications of our actions. It encourages us to make changes that are good for us and our wider environment and community.

Chapter 13: NLP Strategies for Personal Change

13.1 The Change Personal History Technique

The Change Personal History Technique is a compelling Neuro-Linguistic Programming (NLP) approach designed for personal transformation. This technique is grounded in the understanding that our past experiences significantly shape our current perceptions, behaviours, and emotional responses. We can change our present and future selves by altering our internal representation of these past experiences.

Understanding the Technique: The Change Personal History Technique operates on the premise that while we cannot change the actual events of our past, we can change how we perceive and emotionally relate to them. It's about reinterpreting our past experiences, particularly those that have led to limiting beliefs or negative emotional patterns.

Steps of the Technique

1. **Identifying the Target Experience:** Begin by identifying an experience that has contributed to a current limiting belief or negative emotion. This could be an event from childhood, adolescence, or adulthood.

2. **Analyzing the Experience:** Examine the experience and identify its negative beliefs or emotions. Understand the impact of these beliefs on your current behaviour and emotional state.

3. **Reframing the Experience:** Employing NLP reframing techniques changes the narrative of the experience. This involves looking at the event from different perspectives or finding positive aspects and learnings from it.

4. **Altering Submodalities:** Change the memory's submodalities (sensory qualities). If the memory is vivid and distressing, make it dimmer, smaller, or more distant. Altering these sensory qualities can significantly reduce the emotional impact of the memory.

5. **Anchoring Positive Emotions:** Create new, positive associations with the memory. This can be done by anchoring positive emotions or feelings to the memory, essentially overlaying the negative emotions with positive ones.

> **Example:** Application of the Change Personal History Technique

Chapter 13

Step 1: Identifying the Target Experience

Emma's Challenge: Emma has a deep-rooted fear of failure, tracing back to a high school incident where she failed a significant exam. This experience has overshadowed her self-confidence in her professional life.

Step 2: Analyzing the Experience

In Step 2, Emma's realisation comes from introspection and connecting her fear of failure to her experience. She reflects on her emotional responses to challenges at work and recognises a pattern linked to the anxiety and feelings she had during her high school exam failure. This self-awareness helps her identify the high school incident as the root cause of her fear of failure.

Insight: Emma realises that this past failure has led her to believe she is incompetent enough, affecting her willingness to take on new challenges at work.

Step 3: Reframing the Experience

Reframing Action: Emma rethinks the incident, viewing it as an early life lesson in resilience and the value of perseverance. She says, *"That experience taught me the importance of persistence and learning from mistakes."*

Step 4: Altering Submodalities

Altering the Memory: Emma changes her memory's sensory details. She imagines the scene as less colourful, the classroom sounds become muffled, and she sees the event as if it's happening through a foggy lens.

Step 5: Anchoring Positive Emotions

Creating New Associations: Emma recalls a recent successful project at work where she received a commendation. She focuses on the feelings of achievement and pride she felt during that moment. Then, she mentally connects these positive emotions to her high school exam memory.

Result: After working through these steps, Emma notices a profound change. The memory of the high school exam no longer holds a grip of fear over her. It's now a distant, more neutral memory. She feels more confident at work and is more open to taking on tasks.

13.2 Submodalities for Shifting Experience

Submodalities are the fine distinctions or the specific qualities of our internal representations in our mind's eye. They are to our senses what pixels are to a digital image. Think about brightness, size, distance, or colour for visual submodalities. Auditory submodalities include volume, pitch, tempo, and tone, while kinesthetic (feeling) submodalities can be pressure, temperature, or texture.

Using Submodalities for Emotional Shift

The power of submodalities lies in their ability to change the intensity and impact of our experiences. By altering these submodalities, we can change how we feel about a memory or a thought.

1. **Identifying the Submodalities:** Begin by recalling an experience that evokes strong emotion. Notice the submodalities of this experience. Is it a vivid or a dim image? Is the sound loud or soft? Is the feeling intense or mild?

2. **Altering the Experience:** Start experimenting by changing these submodalities. If it's a negative experience, you might make the image smaller, push it further away, or reduce the volume of any associated sounds. For positive experiences, you might do the opposite to enhance the feelings of positivity.

3. **Observing the Emotional Shift:** Notice how altering the submodalities changes your emotional response to the experience. Often, you'll find that the emotional intensity decreases for negative experiences or increases for positive ones.

Example in Practice

Let's consider an example. Emily has a memory of a past failure that often causes her anxiety. She visualises this memory vividly and hears critical voices loudly in her mind.

> **Identifying:** Emily identifies the submodalities: the image is significant and close, and the voices are loud and harsh.

> **Altering:** She then consciously dims the image, makes it smaller, and pushes it further away. She turns down the volume of the voices and changes their tone to something less intimidating.

> **Observing:** After these changes, Emily notices that her anxiety regarding this memory has significantly decreased. The memory feels less immediate and less distressing.

Submodalities are crucial to how we internally represent experiences and, consequently, how we react to them emotionally. By altering these submodalities, we can gain greater control over our emotional responses, enhancing emotional well-being and personal transformation. This technique offers a practical and effective way to shift our experiences, making it a valuable tool in pursuing personal change and growth.

13.3 The New Behavior Generator

Following the exploration of submodalities for shifting experiences, another powerful NLP technique that aids in personal development is the New Behavior Generator. This technique is designed to help individuals adopt new, more beneficial behaviours by utilising the power of visualisation and mental rehearsal.

Understanding the New Behavior Generator

The New Behavior Generator is based on the principle that the brain can't fully distinguish between a vividly imagined experience and an actual one. By vividly imagining ourselves performing a new behaviour, we can create neural pathways that make the actual performance of this behaviour more natural and effortless.

Steps of the New Behavior Generator

1. **Identifying the Desired Behavior:** Identify a specific behaviour you wish to adopt. This could be anything from being more assertive in meetings to staying calm in stressful situations.

2. **Creating a Vivid Mental Image:** Visualize performing this behaviour where you typically want to exhibit it. Make this visualisation as detailed as possible, incorporating submodalities like sight, sound, and feeling.

3. **First-Person and Third-Person Perspectives:** Start by visualising the scenario from a third-person perspective, like watching yourself on a movie screen. Then, switch to a first-person perspective, seeing through your own eyes, and fully immerse yourself in the experience.

4. **Adding Positive Submodalities:** Enhance the visualisation by making it more vivid and adding positive submodalities. For example, if you visualise yourself being assertive, see yourself speaking confidently, hear the muscular tone of your voice, and feel a sense of confidence in your body.

5. **Mental Rehearsal:** Repeatedly rehearse this behaviour mentally. The more you practice it in your mind, the more ingrained it becomes in your neural pathways.

6. **Incorporating Feedback:** Imagine potential challenges and how you would overcome them. You can adjust your behaviour in your visualisation based on this imagined feedback.

Consider the case of Liam, who wants to improve his skills in shooting videos and speaking confidently on camera for his vlog. He is aware that he often appears nervous and hesitant, affecting his content quality.

1. **Identifying the Desired Behavior:** Liam aims to appear relaxed, confident, and engaging while talking on camera.

2. **Creating a Vivid Mental Image:** Liam starts by visualising himself, setting up his camera, standing before it, and beginning to speak. He first sees himself from a third-person perspective, noting his confident posture and expressive hand gestures.

3. **First-Person and Third-Person Perspectives:** After observing himself confidently from an external viewpoint, Liam switches to a first-person perspective. He imagines looking into the camera lens, feeling calm and composed, hearing the clarity in his voice, and experiencing a sense of engagement with his imagined audience.

4. **Adding Positive Submodalities:** To enhance the visualisation, Liam adds details like the warmth of the studio lights, the sound of his clear and steady voice on the microphone, and the feeling of excitement about sharing his ideas.

5. **Mental Rehearsal:** Liam mentally rehearses this scenario repeatedly, each time feeling more at ease with the process of shooting videos and speaking on camera. He imagines different topics he might discuss and how he would interact with the camera in each scenario.

6. **Incorporating Feedback:** He also visualises potential challenges, such as technical issues or forgetting his lines, and sees himself handling these situations smoothly and positively.

After several sessions of practising this visualisation, Liam noticed a significant improvement in his real-life video shoots. He feels more natural and relaxed in front of the camera, and his audience responds positively to his more confident and engaging demeanour.

NLP Strategies for Personal Change

Chapter 14: Modeling Excellence

Modelling Excellence stands as a cornerstone strategy for personal and professional growth. This chapter delves into how NLP's Modeling Excellence can be a transformative tool for individuals seeking to replicate the success of others in their own lives.

14.1 The NLP Strategy for Modeling Success

Modelling in NLP involves observing and replicating the behaviours, thought patterns, and emotional states of those who excel in a particular skill or area. The underlying principle is that one can achieve similar outcomes by emulating the strategies of successful individuals.

1. **Identifying the Model:** Identify someone who excels in the area you wish to improve. This could be a public figure, a colleague, or even a historical figure.

2. **Decoding Excellence:** Analyze the specific behaviours, mindset, and emotional patterns contributing to this person's success. This involves breaking down their methods into replicable steps.

3. **Adapting and Applying:** Once you understand these strategies, adapt them to your context and apply them in your life. This step requires personalisation, as direct imitation is less effective than adaptation.

14.2 Case Studies of Successful Modeling

1. **Business Leadership:** Consider a case study of a junior manager who modelled the leadership style of a renowned CEO. By studying the CEO's decision-making process, communication style, and emotional intelligence, the junior manager incorporated these elements into their leadership approach, significantly improving team performance and personal career advancement.

2. **Sports Performance:** Another case study could involve an athlete who models an Olympic champion's training regimen and mental preparation strategies. By adapting these techniques to their routine, the athlete sees notable improvements in their performance.

14.3 Creating Your Pathway to Excellence

Steps:

1. **Self-Assessment:** Begin by assessing your current skills and identifying specific areas for improvement.

2. **Selecting a Role Model:** Choose a role model who embodies excellence in the area you wish to improve. This selection should be based on thorough research and alignment with your goals.

3. **Deep Observation and Analysis:** Conduct a detailed study of your role model's methods. This involves researching their background, understanding their approach, and, if possible, observing them in action.

4. **Skill Breakdown and Practice:** Break down the skills into manageable components and practice them systematically. This step is crucial for internalising the learned behaviours.

5. **Feedback and Refinement:** Continuously seek feedback on your performance and refine your approach based on this input.

6. **Consistent Application:** Consistently apply these learned behaviours in your daily life or professional activities, making necessary adjustments.

Modelling Excellence in NLP is not merely imitating but understanding and embodying the principles that lead to success in any field. By carefully selecting role models, analysing their success strategies, and adapting these strategies to their own lives, individuals can create their pathway to excellence. This approach offers a structured and effective way to achieve personal growth and success by leveraging the wisdom and experience of those who have already achieved what we aspire.

Chapter 15: Integration and Continuous Improvement

This chapter will explore integrating NLP techniques into daily life, ensure ongoing development through NLP practices, and craft a personal NLP growth plan for sustained progress.

15.1 Integrating NLP into Daily Life

Integrating NLP into everyday life involves making its principles and techniques a natural part of your thought processes, communication style, and approach to challenges. You can start by incorporating simple NLP techniques into your routine. This could be as straightforward as using positive language, practising rapport-building in conversations or employing visualisation techniques for upcoming tasks. Be mindful of opportunities to apply NLP in everyday scenarios, whether managing stress, improving communication with family and colleagues, or setting personal goals.

Focus on forming habits that embed NLP practices into your life. This could involve regular journaling to track progress or setting aside time for meditation and mental rehearsals. Here are some strategies to help maintain focus and successfully integrate these habits:

1. **Start Small and Specific:** Begin with small, manageable NLP practices. For example, start using positive affirmations each morning or practise deep breathing techniques for a few minutes daily. Specificity in your habits makes them easier to remember and follow.

2. **Routine Integration:** Integrate NLP practices into your daily routine. If you already have a morning or bedtime routine, add a brief NLP exercise to this established pattern. This could be as simple as visualising your day ahead with positive outcomes or reflecting on the day's events in the evening using NLP framing techniques.

3. **Use Reminders and Cues:** Set reminders on your phone or place visual cues in your environment that prompt you to practice your NLP habits. For instance, a sticky note on your computer could remind you to practice positive self-talk or empathetic listening during your workday.

4. **Track Your Progress:** Keep a journal or log to track your progress. Recording your experiences with NLP practices helps maintain focus and allows you to see your growth over time. This can be a great motivator.

5. **Consistency is Key:** Consistency is crucial for habit formation. Try to practice your NLP habits at the same time and place each day to reinforce the routine.

6. **Accountability Partners:** Having someone to share your progress with can significantly enhance your focus. Whether

it's a friend, family member, or a colleague, sharing your goals and progress can provide an extra layer of accountability and encouragement.

7. **Celebrate Small Wins:** Acknowledge and celebrate your successes, no matter how small. This positive reinforcement can boost your motivation to maintain your NLP habits.
8. **Mindfulness and Self-Reflection:** Regularly engage in mindfulness and self-reflection to stay aware of your thoughts and behaviours. This awareness can help you remain focused on your NLP practices and recognise areas for improvement.
9. **Flexibility and Adaptation:** Adapt your habits as your life and circumstances change. Flexibility ensures that your NLP practices remain relevant and aligned with your current goals and needs.

15.2 Continuous Improvement through NLP Practices

Continual development is crucial. It's about constantly refining and expanding your skills.

1. **Seek Feedback:** Regularly seek constructive feedback from trusted individuals on your communication and behaviour. You can use this feedback to fine-tune your NLP techniques.
2. **Stay Informed:** Keep up-to-date with the latest developments in NLP. This can involve reading books, attending workshops, or joining NLP forums and discussion groups.
3. **Reflect and Adapt:** Regularly reflect on your experiences with NLP. Analyse if the techniques you're using are effective. Do they need adjustment? Self-reflection is critical to continuous improvement.

15.3 Developing a Personal NLP Growth Plan

Creating a personalised NLP growth plan is about setting a clear path for your development with specific, achievable goals.

1. **Set Clear Objectives:** Identify what you want to achieve with NLP, whether improving certain skills, changing specific behaviours, or attaining particular goals.

2. **Create a Roadmap:** Develop a step-by-step plan for how you will achieve these objectives. This might include specific practices you'll adopt, books you'll read, or courses you'll attend.

3. **Establish Milestones:** Set regular milestones to track your progress. These could be monthly or quarterly check-ins where you assess your development and make any necessary adjustments to your plan.

4. **Seek Mentorship or Coaching:** Consider engaging with an NLP coach or mentor who can guide you through your growth journey, offering expertise and accountability.

5. **Flexible and Dynamic Approach:** Your growth plan should adapt as you progress and your goals evolve.

Creating a personalised NLP growth plan is a strategic approach to achieving specific objectives. Let's explore three examples of such strategies tailored to different goals: adopting a sporty and healthy lifestyle, supporting a partner in a relationship, and increasing earnings.

> **Example 1:** NLP Growth Plan for a Sporty and Healthy Lifestyle
>
> **Objective:** To adopt a consistent exercise routine and healthy eating habits.

Integration and Continuous Improvement

1. **Submodalities for Motivation:** Use NLP submodalities to enhance exercise and healthy eating motivation. Visualise yourself enjoying a workout and savouring healthy meals. Make these images bright and appealing.

2. **Anchoring Positive States:** Create anchors for feelings of vitality and energy you experience after exercising or eating healthily. Use these anchors to trigger motivation when it's time to exercise or choose a meal.

3. **Reframing Obstacles:** Use reframing to view challenges (like skipping a workout or craving unhealthy foods) as opportunities to strengthen your willpower and commitment.

4. **SMART Goals:** Set specific, measurable, achievable, relevant, and time-bound goals, such as *"Jog for 30 minutes every morning"* or *"Prepare a healthy meal plan every week."*

5. **Modeling Excellence:** Identify and model the habits of individuals who successfully maintain a healthy lifestyle. Implement their strategies into your routine, such as meal prepping or morning workouts.

Example 2: NLP Growth Plan for Supporting a Partner

Objective: To be more supportive and understanding in a relationship.

---

1. **Active Listening Techniques:** Practice active listening in conversations with your partner, using techniques like mirroring and paraphrasing to show understanding and empathy.

2. **Positive Affirmations:** Develop affirmations reinforcing your commitment to support, such as *"I am attentive and responsive to my partner's needs."*

3. **Anchoring Positive Emotions:** Create anchors associated with feelings of love and connection. Use these when interacting with your partner, especially in challenging times.

4. **Visualizing Desired Outcomes:** Regularly visualise scenarios where you successfully support your partner, focusing on the emotions and outcomes of these situations.

5. **Feedback and Adaptation:** Please always seek feedback from your partner on your supportiveness and adapt your behaviours accordingly.

Example 3: NLP Growth Plan for Increasing Earnings

Objective: To increase earnings through career advancement or additional income streams.

---

1. **Goal Visualization:** Visualize achieving your financial goals. See yourself receiving a promotion, excelling in a side business, or hitting financial targets.

2. **Modeling Financial Success:** Identify and model the behaviours and mindsets of financially successful individuals. Understand their decision-making processes, risk management, and work ethics.

3. **Positive Language Patterns:** Use language patterns that reflect confidence and success in your professional abilities. Replace any negative self-talk with affirmations related to your financial goals.

4. **Well-Formed Outcomes:** Use the Well-Formed Outcomes technique to set specific financial goals, ensuring they are aligned with your values and long-term objectives.

5. **Continuous Learning and Skill Development:** Set a plan for skill enhancement and learning, crucial for career growth and developing additional income sources.

Integrating NLP into everyday life and the commitment to continuous improvement are essential for anyone seeking to fully harness the power of NLP for personal and professional growth. By mindfully applying NLP techniques in daily scenarios, staying engaged in lifelong learning, and following a tailored growth plan, individuals can achieve profound transformations and steadily progress towards their ultimate goals. This approach ensures that NLP is not just a set of tools and techniques but a living, evolving practice that continually enhances all aspects of your life.

Conclusion: The NLP Journey

As we conclude this exploration into the diverse and transformative world of Neuro-Linguistic Programming (NLP), we must reflect on our journey. NLP is not just a collection of techniques and strategies; it's a mindset, a way of perceiving and interacting with the world that can lead to profound personal and professional growth.

Recap of Key Learnings

Throughout this journey, we've delved into various facets of NLP, from understanding and harnessing the power of language and thought to modelling excellence and integrating NLP into everyday life. Key learnings include:

- The ability to reframe our perspectives, turning challenges into opportunities for growth.
- Techniques like the Swish Pattern and the Change Personal History Technique show us how to alter limiting beliefs and negative emotional patterns.
- The importance of clear and effective communication, enhanced through NLP's insightful approaches like the Meta-Model and the Milton Model.
- The power of modelling success, offering a pathway to replicate the achievements of those we admire.

Staying Engaged with NLP

To continue reaping the benefits of NLP, staying engaged with its practices is crucial. This involves:

- Regular practice and application of NLP techniques in daily life.
- Continuous learning through reading, attending workshops, and engaging with the NLP community.
- Reflect on personal experiences with NLP, understand what works, and make adjustments as needed.

Next Steps and Resources

As you move forward, consider these steps to deepen your NLP practice. You can choose actions that you tend to follow. If you want to keep it secret, there is one way. Only you, books, and perhaps the coach should be involved then. If you wish for the new surroundings of mind mates, there is another approach: find the groups to join and discuss experience.

But for both cases, I strongly recommend two following steps:

1. **Set Personal Goals:** Use NLP techniques to achieve meaningful personal and professional goals. Regularly review and adjust these goals as you grow and learn.
2. **Personal NLP Project:** Start a personal project by applying NLP techniques to a specific area of your life or a new challenge you want to tackle.

Final Thoughts

It's a path of continuous discovery, learning, and application. As you integrate NLP into your life, you'll find it becomes more than just a set of tools – it becomes a part of who you are, influencing how you think, communicate, and act. Embrace this journey with openness, curiosity, and a willingness to grow, and you'll discover NLP's profound impact on your life.

88 Antimanipulation approaches

Understanding and implementing antimanipulation approaches is crucial today, where subtle and not-so-subtle forms of manipulation permeate many aspects of life, from personal relationships to professional environments. Individuals empower themselves by learning to recognise and counteract these tactics, enhancing their emotional and mental resilience. This comprehensive list of manipulation techniques and practical counterstrategies is vital for navigating interactions with greater awareness and confidence. It helps identify potential manipulative behaviours and offers clear, actionable steps to respond effectively. This knowledge is invaluable for maintaining personal integrity, fostering healthy relationships, and making decisions in one's best interest. In essence, it's about reclaiming control over one's choices and interactions in a world where manipulation often goes unnoticed.

MANIPULATION	RESPONSE
1. Gaslighting The manipulator denies or twists reality to make the victim doubt their own memory or perception.	Trust your own memory and perceptions. Seek external validation if needed, and maintain a record of events or conversations.
2. Love Bombing Overwhelming someone with affection and attention to gain control or influence.	Set boundaries, and be wary of overly intense early relationship behaviours.
3. Triangulation Bringing a third person into the dynamics of a relationship creates tension or jealousy.	Communicate directly with the involved parties and refuse to engage in comparisons or competition.
4. Projection Accusing others of their own negative traits or behaviours.	Distinguish between valid criticism and projection. Avoid absorbing or internalising false accusations.

5. Negging Subtle insults or backhanded compliments undermine the victim's self-esteem. The aim is to create a dynamic where the recipient needs approval or validation from the person who commented.	*Recognising the backhanded compliment or subtle insult is crucial, as is responding calmly and confidently to show awareness, reminding yourself of your value without seeking their approval, clarifying that such comments are unacceptable, and considering reducing or ending contact if negging persists.*
6. Feigned Helplessness Pretending inability to do something to make others do it for them.	*Encourage and allow them to handle their own responsibilities unless genuine help is needed.*
7. Guilt Tripping Making someone feel guilty for controlling or manipulating them.	*Recognise emotional manipulation and assert your right to make decisions without undue guilt.*
8. Isolation Cutting off the victim's support network to increase dependence.	*Maintain diverse relationships and social networks. Reach out to friends and family regularly.*
9. Moving Goalposts Continuously changing demands or expectations.	*Set clear, consistent boundaries and expectations. Avoid chasing ever-changing goals.*
10. Selective Attention Giving or withholding attention and affection to manipulate emotions.	*Recognise this pattern and seek emotional stability and validation from within or from reliable sources.*
11. Bait and Switch Promising one thing but delivering something else to manipulate or deceive.	*Clarify expectations upfront. If the outcome differs significantly, address the discrepancy directly.*

12. Silent Treatment Refusing to communicate to exert control or inflict emotional pain.	*Maintain your self-esteem and reach out for external support. Don't let silence coerce you into compliance.*
13. Overwhelm with Jargon Using complex language or technical terms to confuse or intimidate.	*Ask for clarification in simpler terms. Don't be afraid to admit when you don't understand something.*
14. False Consensus Pretending that a viewpoint or desire is widely shared when it isn't, to pressure someone to conform.	*Research and validate claims independently. Trust your perspective, even if it differs from the alleged consensus.*
15. Victim Playing Exaggerating or fabricating hardship to gain sympathy or manipulate others into providing support or concessions.	*Be empathetic, but set boundaries. Offer support in ways that encourage self-sufficiency.*
16. Scarcity Tactic Creating a false sense of urgency or rarity to pressure a decision or action.	*Take time to make decisions, especially under pressure. Assess the actual urgency or need independently.*
17. Flattery Using excessive praise to disarm or manipulate someone into compliance.	*Enjoy compliments but remain aware of their potential use as a manipulation tool. Keep decisions objective.*
18. Double Bind Offering two choices that lead to the same outcome, removing real choice.	*Recognise the false dilemma. Seek or create alternatives that provide genuine choice.*
19. Fearmongering Using fear to manipulate others into action or compliance.	*Question the basis of the fear. Seek information from diverse, reliable sources to understand the real risk.*

20. Hypercriticism
Continually finding fault or critiquing to erode someone's confidence.

Distinguish between constructive feedback and manipulation. Affirm your self-worth and reject unjust criticism.

21. Excessive Complaining
Constant complaining to garner sympathy or manipulate others into solving their problems.

Offer support but encourage problem-solving and personal responsibility. Avoid becoming an enabler of dependency.

22. Intimidation
Using threats or aggressive behaviour to coerce or frighten someone into compliance.

Stand firm in your boundaries. Seek help if safety is a concern. Do not engage in confrontation.

23. Mirroring and Matching
Imitating someone's behaviour or preferences to gain trust or approval.

Be aware of excessive mimicry. Trust should be based on genuine interactions, not just mirrored behaviours.

24. Bandwagon Pressure
Suggesting that 'everyone is doing it' as a way to pressure someone into compliance.

Make decisions based on your values and information, not just what others do.

25. Oversharing
Sharing too much personal information creates a false sense of intimacy and trust.

Set personal boundaries. Share information at a pace and level that feels comfortable for you.

26. Selective Memory
Conveniently forgetting commitments or conversations when it suits their agenda.

Keep records of important agreements. Gently remind and confront discrepancies in their recall.

27. Withholding Information
Intentionally omitting or withholding important information to manipulate a situation or decision.

Seek comprehensive information before making decisions. Ask direct questions to uncover any withheld details.

28. Overpromising Making grand promises to influence behaviour with no intention of following through.	*Judge by actions, not words. Be wary of promises that seem too good to be true.*
29. Undermining Subtly weakening someone's position, confidence, or status to gain the advantage.	*Stay confident in your abilities. Seek feedback from trusted sources to counteract any undermining.*
30. Scapegoating Blaming someone else for problems to deflect responsibility or scrutiny.	*Look for evidence before accepting blame. Encourage accountability and fact-based assessments.*
31. Cherry-Picking Data Selectively presenting data or facts to mislead or persuade.	*Research independently to get the whole picture. Question the context and completeness of the information presented.*
32. Social Proof Manipulation Using the behaviour of others, often fabricated or exaggerated, to influence someone's actions or beliefs.	*Make decisions based on objective evidence and personal principles, not just others' actions or opinions.*
33. Rationalisation Providing seemingly logical, reasonable explanations or excuses for behaviour that may have other, often less justifiable, motives.	*Look beyond surface explanations. Evaluate actions and patterns, not just the rationalisations that are given.*
34. Playing the Martyr Portraying themselves as self-sacrificing to manipulate others into feeling indebted or guilty.	*Acknowledge their efforts, but don't let guilt influence your decisions. Maintain healthy boundaries.*
35. Indirect Communication Hinting or implying rather than stating directly, often to avoid responsibility.	*Acknowledge their efforts, but don't let guilt influence your decisions. Maintain healthy boundaries.*

36. Excessive Dependency Relying too much on someone else for emotional support, decision-making, or validation, often to control or manipulate them.	*Encourage independence and personal responsibility. Set boundaries to maintain a healthy balance in the relationship.*
37. Sudden Changes of Heart Unexpectedly changing opinions or plans to catch others off guard and manipulate the situation.	*Adapt flexibly but maintain your core principles and goals. Don't be swayed by sudden, unexplained shifts.*
38. Gaslighting through Denial Consistently denying facts, events, or statements to make others question their reality or memory.	*Trust your perceptions and records. Seek proof and external confirmation if needed.*
39. False Dichotomy Presenting two opposing options as the only possibilities when others exist.	*Look for alternative options. Don't be constrained by artificially limited choices.*
40. Emotional Blackmail Using emotional vulnerability or sensitive information to control or manipulate.	*Recognise emotional manipulation. Set firm boundaries around emotional well-being and personal information.*
41. Exaggeration or Minimization Dramatically overstating or understating facts or situations to manipulate perceptions.	*Seek objective information. Compare their statements with known facts and context.*
42. Selective Inattention Deliberately ignoring certain facts or details to push a particular narrative or agenda.	*Pay attention to what is not being said or shown. Look for a more complete and balanced understanding.*

43. Emotional Overload
This involves overwhelming someone with intense emotional expressions or drama to cloud their judgement and influence their decisions. It's a tactic where the manipulator uses strong emotional displays to distract or pressure the other person.

In such situations, it's essential to take a step back to think logically and not make decisions solely based on the emotional intensity of the moment.

44. Labeling
Assigning a label or stereotype to discredit or oversimplify someone's position.

Reject unfair labels. Focus on the substance of the discussion, not just on how it's framed.

45. Preemptive Defense
Making excuses in advance to deflect potential criticism or failure.

Focus on actual results and behaviour. Don't let preemptive excuses lower accountability.

46. Forced Teaming
Creating a sense of partnership or shared destiny to manipulate someone into cooperation.

Assess the actual level of shared interest or goals. Maintain independence in decision-making.

47. False Compromise
Pretending to make concessions and compromises that are actually in the manipulator's favour creates an illusion of fairness.

Critically evaluate all 'compromises' to ensure they are genuinely fair and equitable. Don't be swayed by the mere appearance of compromise.

48. Ingratiation
Excessive flattery or acts of kindness to gain favour or compliance.

Appreciate genuine kindness but be wary of manipulation. Make decisions based on objective criteria.

49. Hypotheticals
Using imaginary scenarios to manipulate emotions or decisions.

Stay grounded in reality. Don't base decisions on hypothetical and unverified situations.

50. Divide and Conquer Creating or exploiting divisions among others to gain power or control.	*Seek direct communication and collaboration. Don't let third-party claims create unnecessary conflict.*
51. Ambiguity Using vague or ambiguous language to avoid commitment or to mislead.	*Ask for clarification and specific details. Don't base decisions on ambiguous statements.*
52. Appeal to Authority Using authority figures or experts (real or fabricated) to sway opinion or decisions.	*Verify credentials and the relevance of the authority. Rely on your judgment and additional sources.*
53. Playing Dumb Pretending not to understand or be unaware of something to avoid responsibility or manipulate outcomes.	*Provide clear information. If needed, repeat or rephrase to ensure understanding and accountability.*
54. Victimization Narrative Portraying themselves as a perpetual victim to gain sympathy or manipulate others.	*Be empathetic, but look for patterns of behaviour. Encourage problem-solving and personal responsibility.*
55. Over-Identification Excessively identifying with a group, cause, or ideology to manipulate or gain trust.	*Be cautious of overzealous identification, primarily if used to justify questionable actions or beliefs.*
56. Moral High Ground Assuming a position of moral superiority to manipulate or shame others into compliance.	*Acknowledge valid points, but don't be intimidated by moral grandstanding. Stick to your ethical principles.*
57. Pathologizing Labelling normal behaviour or opinions as pathological to undermine or control.	*Trust your understanding of normal behaviour. Seek second opinions if necessary.*

58. Rewriting History Changing the story of past events to benefit their narrative or position.	*Rely on documented facts and your recollections. Challenge inconsistencies in their narrative.*
59. Inconsistent Standards Frequently changing the criteria or rules to keep someone uncertain and off-balance makes it difficult for them to meet expectations or argue effectively.	*Identify and challenge the inconsistency in standards. Seek to establish and agree upon clear, stable criteria or rules.*
60. Feigning Offense Pretending to be offended or hurt to manipulate a situation or conversation.	*Be respectful, but question the authenticity of the offence, mainly if it's used to derail or control discussions.*
61. All-or-Nothing Thinking Presenting situations as black-and-white, with no middle ground, to force a decision or viewpoint.	*Seek and propose nuanced perspectives. Avoid extreme positions unless they are truly the only options.*
62. Catastrophizing Exaggerating the negative consequences of an action or event to induce fear or compliance.	*Assess risks realistically. Challenge exaggerated claims by seeking factual information.*
63. False Altruism Pretending to act in someone's best interest while actually pursuing their own agenda.	*Evaluate the actions and outcomes, not just the stated intentions. Look for underlying motives.*
64. Straw Man Argument Misrepresenting someone's argument to make it easier to attack or discredit.	*Clarify your original position. Refuse to engage with the misrepresented version.*

65. Forced Teamwork
Insisting on working together, often under the guise of collaboration, to gain control or influence.

Evaluate the necessity and benefits of collaboration. Set clear boundaries and roles in teamwork.

66. Hasty Generalization
Making a broad conclusion based on limited or insufficient evidence.

Ask for more evidence. Don't accept generalisations without substantial support.

67. Slippery Slope
Suggesting a minor first step will lead to a chain of related (often negative) events.

Challenge the likelihood of the proposed chain of events. Decide based on realistic probabilities.

68. Ad Hominem Attacks
Attacking the person making an argument, rather than the argument itself, to discredit them.

Refocus the conversation on the argument. Don't engage in personal attacks.

69. Appeal to Tradition
Arguing that something must be done a certain way because it has always been done that way.

Consider the merits of the current method, but be open to innovation and improvement.

70. Overgeneralization
Making a sweeping statement based on a single event or insufficient evidence.

Look for additional examples or evidence. Avoid basing decisions on overgeneralised statements.

71. False Equivalence
Equating two unrelated things to justify a point or action.

Question the validity of the comparison. Look for logical inconsistencies in the equivalence.

72. Appeal to Fear
Using fear to motivate behaviour or belief, often exaggerating potential dangers.

Evaluate the actual risk independently. Make decisions based on facts, not fear.

73. Selective Outrage Expressing disproportionate anger or indignation about specific issues to manipulate opinion or action.	*Recognise when outrage is being used as a tool. Seek balanced perspectives on the issue.*
74. Bandwagoning Encouraging a course of action because it's popular or trendy.	*Make decisions based on merit and personal values, not just on popularity. Fashion changes, but values are internal, often unconscious goals, and you will be happier following them.*
75. Circular Reasoning Using a statement to prove itself creates a logical loop without real evidence.	*Look for actual evidence. Don't accept circular arguments that lack independent support.*
76. Appeal to Novelty Arguing that something is superior simply because it is new or modern.	*Assess the actual merits, not just the novelty. New doesn't always mean better.*
77. False Anecdotal Evidence Using personal stories or isolated examples instead of sound evidence to argue a point.	*Look for statistically significant evidence. Don't base conclusions on anecdotal data alone.*
78. Sunk Cost Fallacy Arguing to continue a course of action simply because of the investment already made.	*Make decisions based on future benefits, not past investments.*
79. Appeal to Ignorance Claiming something is true because it hasn't been proven false, or vice versa.	*Seek positive evidence for claims. A lack of evidence is not proof of anything.*

80. Victory by Definition Defining terms in a biased way guarantees they can only win the argument.	*Challenge and clarify definitions. Ensure terms are used fairly and consistently.*
81. Appeal to Pity Using sympathy or pity to influence decisions or opinions.	*Be empathetic, but make decisions based on objective criteria rather than emotional appeals.*
82. Over-Simplification Reducing complex situations to overly simple terms to manipulate understanding or outcome.	*Recognise the complexity of situations. Avoid making decisions based on oversimplified explanations.*
83. Post Hoc Rationalization Suggesting that because one event follows another, the first must cause the second.	*Look for actual causal relationships. Don't assume causation just because of sequence.*
84. Euphemisms Using mild or vague terms to disguise unpleasant or offensive realities.	*Clarify the actual meaning. Don't be misled by soft language.*
85. Appeal to Incredulity Arguing that something must be false because it's difficult to believe.	*Base beliefs on evidence, not on the ease of understanding or belief.*
86. False Inevitability Claiming something is inevitable to discourage resistance or encourage acceptance.	*Challenge the inevitability. Explore alternative outcomes and possibilities.*
87. Diversion Changing the topic to avoid answering questions or addressing critical issues.	*Notice when conversations are being diverted. Steer them back to the original point.*

88. Micro-Managing
Overly controlling or scrutinising every tiny detail of someone's actions or work, often to exert dominance or control.

Assert your competence and right to work with reasonable autonomy. Address the issue directly if micro-managing becomes excessive.

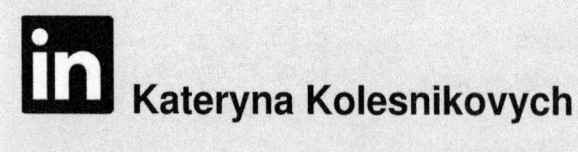

in Kateryna Kolesnikovych

Please do not hesitate to contact me
katerynakolesnikovych@gmail.com

Resources

Various resources are available to enrich your journey with neurolinguistic programming (NLP). These resources can provide deeper insights, practical tools, and ongoing support as you explore and apply NLP principles.

Books and Literature

1. *"Frogs into Princes"* **by Richard Bandler and John Grinder:** A foundational text that introduces the core concepts of NLP.
2. *"The Structure of Magic"* **by Richard Bandler and John Grinder:** Explores the therapeutic aspects of NLP, particularly the use of language to effect change.
3. *"NLP: The Essential Guide to Neuro-Linguistic Programming"* **by Tom Hoobyar, Tom Dotz, and Susan Sanders:** A comprehensive guide that covers a wide range of NLP topics in an accessible format.
4. *"Change Your Life with NLP"* **by Lindsey Agness:** Focuses on practical applications of NLP in various aspects of personal development.

Online Courses and Workshops

1. **Udemy and Coursera:** Offer various NLP courses, from introductory to advanced levels, taught by experienced practitioners.
2. **Local NLP Training Programs:** Many cities have NLP training centers offering workshops and certification programs.

Websites and Online Forums

1. **The Association for Neuro-Linguistic Programming (ANLP):** Provides resources, a directory of practitioners, and updates on conferences and events.
2. **NLP Reddit Community:** A forum for discussion, advice, and sharing experiences related to NLP.

Podcasts and YouTube Channels

1. **NLP Podcasts:** Such as *"The NLP View"* and *"The Brain Software Podcast with Mike Mandel"* offer insights, interviews, and discussions on various NLP topics.
2. **YouTube Channels:** Channels like *"NLP and Coaching Institute"* provide free videos on NLP techniques and concepts.

Networking and Community Groups

1. **Local Meetup Groups:** Joining NLP Meetup groups can be a great way to connect with other enthusiasts and practitioners.
2. **Professional NLP Associations:** Membership in professional bodies like the International NLP Federation offers networking opportunities and access to professional development resources.

Personal NLP Coaching and Mentoring

1. **Professional Coaches:** Engaging with a certified NLP coach can provide personalised guidance and accelerated learning.

Conferences and Seminars

1. **NLP Conferences:** Annual conferences such as the International NLP Conference provide opportunities to learn from leading experts and network with other practitioners.

Final Note

These resources serve as a gateway to deeper exploration and mastery of NLP. They offer the opportunity to expand your knowledge, connect with a community of learners and practitioners, and stay abreast of the latest developments in the field of NLP. Whether you prefer self-study, online learning, or interactive workshops, a wealth of resources is available to support your journey in NLP.

Printed in Great Britain
by Amazon